Every Bite Affects The World

an earth care cookbook for joyful, mindful eating

*Catherine Verrall
and a host of friends*

By Catherine Verrall
Foreword by Dr. Nettie Wiebe

Foreword by Dr. Nettie Wiebe.
Illustrations © by Erika Folnovic.

Produced by:
FriesenPress
Suite 300 – 852 Fort Street
Victoria, BC, Canada V8W 1H8
www.friesenpress.com

Distributed to the trade by The Ingram Book Company

Printing certified by the Forest Stewardship Council® (FSC™), the Sustainable Forestry Initiative® (SFI®) and the Programme for the Endorsement of Forestry Certification (PEFC™).
POD printing reduces potential printing waste by printing one book at a time.

Table of Contents

Commendations

"This book nourishes hope. And to meet our ecological, economic and moral challenges, a hopeful heart comes first. When asked, "But what can I do?" it is a joy to commend these pages. They will not only strengthen your body and soul, but those of your children and grandchildren as well."

Mardi Tindal, 40th Moderator of the United Church of Canada.

"I read *Every Bite Affects the World* with great interest - so helpful and informative! It is a great education in many ways, but most importantly it clarifies why we need to make better choices for our own health and the environment. I look forward to using this valuable book to inform and change my choices in the future."

Louise Burns-Murray, retired Director of a Women's Shelter.

"This cookbook is a tool we can use as we plan our daily meals. We can learn to eat with increased awareness as to how our choices affect those living in the global South; at the same time strengthening the local economy, and improving our health and the health of our planet."

Maureen Sonntag, member of Development and Peace, and of Kairos.

"Being able to know and see where our food comes from is a luxury in today's world. I am very excited seeing this book because it raises awareness of the many benefits of local, organic food."

Dean Kreutzer, Over the Hill Orchards, Lumsden, Saskatchewan.

To the women and men and children, here and far away, who
work to grow food in harmony with the rhythms of nature

To the well-being of those who will come
after us, "for seven generations"

To the bees and the butterflies, whose
diligent work gives us food and joy

Foreword
by Nettie Wiebe

"What we need to do is to revalue food and food production, and we have to stop this idea that what Nature gives us is for free and hence deserves a low commodity price. We have to start thinking that what Nature gives us is the most precious and is, in fact, the key to our sustainable continued existence in the world." – Nettie Wiebe

The fun of cooking interesting, delicious food is only surpassed by the delight of eating it in good company. These experiences are enriched by knowing where the ingredients came from, or better still, having actually grown some of them in one's own flower pots, garden, fields, pastures or pens. And all of this is enhanced when one can eat with a clear conscience, knowing that this food not only fills those enjoying it but also nourishes the world. As an enthusiastic gardener and cook, an organic farmer and passionate eater, I am pleased to know that these marvelous, important possibilities are being offered to many others through this innovative cookbook.

This book is a recipe book with a difference. It combines the key ingredients of good living: healthy food, love of others, ecological care and political justice. The recipes for eating well are enhanced with notes on how to eat to sustain our own bodies while enhancing life in our communities and around the world.

Food is about relationships. Along with soups, breads, salads, stews, pies and a host of other delicious foods, the aromas wafting from kitchens carry the scents of connections and caring. Connections between what we eat and who we are (our cultural and ethnic identities) and caring for self, families, guests, farmers, water, soil, animal, plant, insect and bird life.

The current trend in cooking, and also in agriculture, has been to "go global." Even if you avoid the expensive, glossy recipe books and upscale restaurants serving exotic foods, most of the items on grocery store shelves have also come from faraway places.

Some imported foods currently displayed in supermarket aisles have serious ecological, economic, political and moral consequences. Food from around the world requires millions of freight miles resulting in tonnes of greenhouse gas emissions. The uniform appearance of millions of kilograms of fresh produce can only be achieved by suppressing Nature's diversity using chemical herbicides, insecticides, fungicides and fertilizers.

These ecological consequences are accompanied by economic and political dynamics. Out of season fresh fruits, vegetables and flowers are only possible if fields and forests elsewhere are diverted from producing food for local people into crops for export. Millions of peasants and small-scale farmers have been impoverished and displaced as land is consolidated and converted into growing commodities for export. This rural displacement represents an incalculable loss of social well-being, family and community integrity and cultural diversity.

Farm communities here on the prairies are also suffering such losses. Caught in the throes of export driven agriculture, with intensified competition and government policies pushing further consolidation, ecological and social costs are discounted in favour of agribusiness profits. It's as if a global, corporate plow wind is flattening shelter-belts, farmsteads, communities, diverse cultures and biodiversity in its path.

Transforming these forces and converting food systems into sustainable, locally controlled, democratic, culturally appropriate and nutritious food systems requires political courage, solidarity and love. This is the struggle for food sovereignty. Peasants, farming families, indigenous peoples and urban citizens, are waging it here in Canada and around the world.

Everyone who eats, shops for groceries or cooks can engage in building food sovereignty.

Joyful, mindful cooking, eating and living begin at home to help serve up a better world!

> **Nettie Wiebe** is a Saskatchewan organic farmer with a PhD in Philosophy. Teacher, writer, speaker, farm organization leader and public policy advocate, she is presently Professor of Church and Society at St. Andrew's College, University of Saskatchewan, and past president of the National Farmers' Union. A member of Via Campesina (International Peasants' Movement) Coordinating Commission, she takes her political activism from a local to a national to a global scale. But first and foremost, she says she is "an eater like all other creatures." Recent books co-edited by Nettie Wiebe are *Food Sovereignty: Reconnecting Food, Nature and Community*. 2010; also, *Food Sovereignty in Canada: Creating Just and Sustainable Food Systems*. 2011.

Introduction
by Catherine Verrall

Every Bite is an Invitation to Relationship.

We are all eaters. We all depend on food. And all food depends on complex relationships with water and air, sun and soil. Plants and creatures live in a constantly changing relationship with each other, with trillions of microscopic beings, with people and with the spiritual Mystery that energizes all. So as we eat, we too enter into that constantly inter-relating web. This book keeps us mindful of these connections, as we prepare and eat our food. When we eat food grown locally – wherever we are – we connect with the land where we live. We build relationships with the farmers who care for the soil and our food. We discover powerful relationships between what we eat, climate chaos and our changing, dying ecosystems. *Every Bite Affects the World* extends our awareness to the people and the earth and the waters from where our far-food comes. And Every Bite connects our eating with our bodies' well-being, generating the Life-Force within us.

Every Bite is an Invitation to Creativity.

It calls us to envision what balanced sustainable life might be like, to find creative ways to make this vision become real. Recipes are just collections of ideas. Be brave enough to mix and match, experiment depending on what you've got and who is eating. Remember: mistakes are new ways of learning! Adventure out to find ingredients new to you, in Farmers' Markets, in regular stores or in Health Food stores. Many community members donated recipes for this book. These recipes have been adjusted and tested to express the book's theme: food that is earth-sustaining: local, organic and fair trade when available; avoiding factory-farmed meat, Genetically Modified (GM) crops, and most processed "food" when possible. *Every Bite* shows the How and the Why. Growing our own food is another creative step, even if it is a few herbs, tomatoes or lettuce plants on patio or balcony, or a small patch in the yard. We do the best we can. It is a journey.

Every Bite is an Invitation to Community.

It grew out of one particular community, a Church congregation, and our World Food Day service titled "Nourishing the World." *Every Bite Affects the World* reaches out for the well-being of all Creation, starting in our kitchens here in Saskatchewan. When we eat healthy food at the table together we can share community with family and friends; so invite a lonely person, a new friend or a family member home for tea or soup – it doesn't have to be fancy. *Every Bite Affects the World* is an invitation to be part of the world-wide up-surging evolutionary movement of people who struggle and rejoice in occupying and re-creating a real food system again.

Eating is not only a survival act.
Eating can be an act of justice-making.
Preparing and eating food can be spiritual encounters.

Namaste (NAH-mas-tay)
The Spirit in me greets the Spirit in you.

EATING

EATING connects us to the Earth.
EATING links us to sun and wind
to waters and bees
and zillions of soil's micro-organisms.
EATING binds us to plants
and animals and fish.
EATING connects us to
people here and far away –
all our fellow eaters
people who laboured to grow
and process and transport and sell
and then prepare our food –
people whose food source is stolen,
in part because we have so much.
EATING unites us with the radiant
energies in all this holy creation
given to all of us eaters, everywhere,
that we might have healthy life.

Health Statement

The information found in this cookbook is intended to help guide readers toward healthier eating choices and conscious ethical food decisions. It is always best practice to consult a medical/health professional before changing your diet regime, especially if you are pregnant or nursing. This book is not inclusive. Any mention of an organization, product, service, company or professional does not imply endorsement by either the author or the publisher. Any adverse effect arising from the use or misuse of the information provided in this book is the sole responsibility of the reader and not that of the author or publisher. The author and recipe contributors have made their best efforts to the best of their abilities in testing each recipe. The author and publisher shall have no liability or responsibility to any person or entity regarding any loss or damage incurred, or alleged to have incurred, directly or indirectly, by the information contained in this book.

In this book, GF (Gluten-Free) means using grains that usually contain no gluten. GF here does not apply to other processed ingredients such as baking powder. Check the label.

GM or GMO means Genetically Modified or Genetically Modified Organism.

Chapter 1:
Food Givers

Indigenous Peoples of the Americas

More than half of all plant foods now eaten in the world were first developed, grown and utilized by the First Peoples of the Americas. As reported by Jack Weatherford in *Indian Givers: How Native Americans Transformed the World,* they were the world's greatest plant breeders of many different varieties of each plant, suited to each environment and need. New World farmers showed the Old World how to plant seeds individually by hand, rather than broadcasting by handfuls over the ground. Indigenous farmers are still teaching researchers how to grow diverse varieties of vegetables. This knowledge could have prevented the Irish potato famine, and could still strengthen our future food security. Yet Indigenous farmers and their vital knowledge and seeds are being destroyed daily by development such as mining, clear-cutting and monoculture plantations, usually benefiting foreign corporations and shareholders.

Common Food Plants first discovered and developed by Indigenous scientist-farmers of the Americas

Amaranth	Arrowroot
Avocado	Beans (the Iroquois developed 60 varieties)
Cashews	Chia seeds
Chilies	Chocolate (cacao)
Corn (maize)	Hickory nut
Hot peppers	Jerusalem artichokes
Maple syrup	Melons
Papaya	Peanuts
Pumpkin	Potatoes (developed about 10,000 years ago, but there are still over 3,000 different types in the Andes)
Quinoa	Squashes
Sunflowers	Sweet peppers
Sweet potatoes	Tapioca
Tomatoes	Vanilla
Wild rice	Yams

Indigenous Peoples also invented many ways to use foods such as berries, crabapples, clams, cranberries, nuts, and wild turkeys.

Corn, Beans and Squash are the Three Sisters of American Indigenous farmers – beans grow up the corn stalk and add nitrogen to the soil, while squash leaves protect the soil – this is also known as companion growing!

Foreign Farm Workers

Farm workers abroad are at far more risk than eaters here. Field workers are exposed to high levels of toxic chemicals and may bring the contaminants home on their clothes to their families, causing skin rashes, birth defects, cancer and other illnesses. This is another reason to avoid imported mass-produced food and to demand fair working conditions for those food givers. Learn more from www.farmworkerjustice.org/content/pesticide-safety and *Pesticide Action Network North America at* www.panna.org/issues/frontline-communities/farmworkers.

Even in Canada, although some are treated with respect, many migrant and immigrant workers on very large farms are vulnerable. They often live in harsh, isolated conditions, are subject to mistreatment, and lack benefits such as sick leave, overtime, adequate health care and other services. They can be exposed to dangerous chemicals, and are denied their basic rights, legal status and respect. Studies show they also experience a high rate of hunger. The film *El Contrato* shows the problems of tomato workers in Leamington, Ontario.

Something to think about: How are unions and governments acting to protect foreign workers, our food givers?

Women in Food-Related Occupations within Canada and Around the World

Women in food-manufacturing occupations in Ontario were found to have a much higher risk of breast cancer before menopause if they work in plastics manufacturing and food canning, due to exposure to BPA in can linings. Women in farming, who are exposed to pesticides and other agricultural chemicals, have less risk, but still 36% higher. Women migrant workers are also subject to sexual harassment.

Women Farmers

"The vast majority of the world's people - 70 percent - earn their livelihood by producing food. The majority of these farmers are women" writes activist-scientist Vandana Shiva, in *Stolen Harvest: The Hijacking of the Global Food Supply.*

Traditionally, and still in the global south, women are the keepers and protectors of seeds – our planet's crop diversity and our climate change security. Women observe, choose and share their seeds. Women's skill feeds and teaches children. Multinational agro-food corporations threaten women even more than men. In developing countries women need more support to do their own sustainable growing. *The Unitarian Service Committee (USC)* and *Oxfam Canada* release good information on this.

To learn more about women farmers in Canada, read "*Transforming Agriculture: Women Farmers Define a Food Sovereignty Policy for Canada*" in Wittman, Desmarais and Wiebe, *Food Sovereignty in Canada*: *Creating Just and Sustainable Food Systems.* Also learn about the crises all Canadian farmers, especially women, are dealing with: crises created mainly by government policies, mono-lithic agro-chemical corporations, as well as climate changes. Learn about their insights for safeguarding food and communities for future generations.

Fair Trade

Certified Fair Trade products guarantee that the foods grown by small farmers in the developing world have gained a minimum fair price for the producers, decent working conditions plus an investment in their communities. Fair Trade encourages organic methods of agri-culture, preserves ecosystems, protects human rights and trade unions, and bans child labour. The Fair Trade movement is based on democratic organization, and aims to transform society's values. This independent international certification is based on yearly inspec-tions. Fair Trade Canada is our independent national, non-profit Fair Trade certification organization. Look for the logo. Fair Trade foods include coffee, tea, cocoa, chocolate chips and bars, various sugars, dried mixed fruit and nut butters that are available in specialty stores. Big business "Fair Trade," a newer development, is better than unfair trade, but produce is grown by minimum standards and not in a co-operative manner.

Chapter 2:
Food Sovereignty

Food Security means having enough safe and nourishing food. This definition might sometimes include some principles of Food Sovereignty but unfortunately the term Food Security is often used to advance agri-business chemicals, monoculture, dispossession of small farmers, and ecological degradation.

Food Sovereignty – or Peoples' Food Sovereignty – centres on the idea that people must reclaim their power of decision-making in the food system by rebuilding the relationships between people and the land and between producers and consumers. Food Sovereignty calls for a shift from food as a commodity to food as a public good, strengthening communities, ecosystems and economics.

La Via Campesina is the transnational grassroots activist movement of small-scale farmers, "people of the land." In 1996 they were the first to use the term "food sovereignty." They are the leading edge of world resistance against industrial agri-business – the corporate take-over of land, food and seeds on which all life depends. Rafael Alegra, a peasant leader from Honduras said *"What unites us is a spirit of transformation and struggle....We aspire to a better world, a more just world where real equality and social justice exist."* La Via Campesina organizations are active in at least 51 countries circling the globe, with many sub-groups in each country. The story of La

Via Campesina has been written by Saskatchewan farmer turned professor, Annette Aurélie Desmarais, in her book *La Via Campesina*. Annette and Nettie Wiebe, former president of the National Farmers' Union, have been involved in the organization from its very beginning.

The Six Pillars of Food Sovereignty were developed by the 2007 International Forum for Food Sovereignty in Mali, West Africa; the Seventh Pillar was added by members of the Indigenous Circle during Food Secure Canada's 2011 People's Food Policy process:

Focuses on Food for People
Values Food Providers
Localizes Food Systems
Puts Control Locally
Builds Knowledge and Skills
Works with Nature
Believes Food is Sacred

An excellent resource is *Toward Food Sovereignty for All* published in 2013 by the United Church of Canada, which states *"Food sovereignty recognizes both the role of women as the primary producers and preparers as well as the value of Indigenous Agricultural systems and traditional knowledge in food production."*

Indigenous Food Sovereignty Movement in Canada: the Indigenous food sovereignty movement in Canada shows a way that could transform the industrial food system toward a more fair and ecological model for all. Everyone can learn from Indigenous knowledge, values, wisdom and practice. Dawn Morrison, writing in *Food Sovereignty in Canada*, outlines the four principles guiding the struggle for Indigenous food sovereignty:

> Food is a sacred gift from the Creator and so the right to food is sacred, along with the sacred responsibilities to nurture healthy, interdependent relationships with the land, plants and animals that provide our food;

> Every individual, family, community and region is called to daily action;

> Food sovereignty means self-determination: freedom from corporate-controlled food, freedom of food giving lands and waters from pollution and other destructive assaults;

> Indigenous food sovereignty attempts to bring together in a restorative way indigenous food and cultural values with mainstream economic activities (forestry, fisheries, conservation, health, agriculture and community development).

Chapter 3:
Eating Local

"Eating locally isn't just a fad – it may be one of the most important ways we save ourselves and the planet."– David Suzuki

In *Every Bite* the term "local" means food sourced close to *our* home, whether it is in the Prairies, the Atlantic Provinces, Ontario, Quebec, British Columbia or Nunavut. It is the food of Indigenous Peoples and of settler populations and its ingredients have not travelled long distances.

As Canada's multicultural identity continues to develop, so do our taste buds! Many of the recipes found in this book express a diverse multicultural zest. Wherever our ancestral home, be it here or elsewhere, we bring recipes to enhance Canadian culture using ingredients found locally, as much as possible. We can also give thanks for the rare treats, such as spices and tropical fruits imported from far-away places and to the workers who produced them. We hope they received fair compensation. But this book encourages readers to support local farmers and discover local food diversity, as close to home as possible.

The activist singing group the Raging Grannies wrote a song:

Eating Local

Sung to the old tune My Grandfather's Clock.

We'll care for the soil as it cares for us
Giving food through all our life long.
We'll care for the worms and waters as they work
In harmony like a song.
NO toxic chemicals poisoning the land
NO erosion from water and wind
But stop, look, and daily give thanks
To all creatures of Earth - our kin.

We'll eat of the food that is grown right here
As the seasons roll around.
We'll support local farmers as they nourish us
Drawing health from our native ground.
Less exotic fruits from far-away climes
Less OUT-of-season veg on our plate.
But stop, look, and daily give thanks
To our farmers. For warm days we can wait.

Remember the workers who toil far away
Their land robbed to grow treats for us.
Remember the pesticides wrecking their health
For our perfect-looking food. Is that just?
NO more food transports pounding down our roads
Polluting the air and the land
But stop, think of the cost to the Earth.
Let's buy what grows close at hand.

Our present food system has gone haywire. Faceless corporate webs control most of our food. Fewer people, in Canada and elsewhere, are able to feed themselves with health-giving food. Much of the food available does not give health. Its production degrades the environment. While far too many people suffer hunger and starvation, nearly half of the food produced world-wide is wasted. Soaring food costs ignite world food riots. Climate change and land pressures spur migration in search of food, fomenting wars. At home, illness and health care costs are surging, non-renewable and dwindling fossil fuels provide the energy that produces and distributes our food supply, while devastating the planet. Climate upheaval and ecosystem collapse are becoming frighteningly real. The more we see the connections, the less we can ignore our unsustainable food system and our own daily connections as we eat.

Eat Local to enjoy fresher, healthier food, grown on the soil of a local farmer, with less, or no toxic additives. Food begins to deteriorate the minute it is picked, so the farther produce has to travel the less nutrition it has by the time it reaches the supermarket and then even less nutrition by the time it is eaten. Most imported produce is picked before the fruit or vegetable is ripened, and sprayed with a preservative chemical to reduce mold and other bacterial growth so it does not spoil as it ages in transport.

Eat Local to strengthen food security in closer, safer, food systems. The average Canadian meal travels 3,000 kilometres to get to our plates, on cheap oil which is becoming scarce. Planes, trucks, ships and trains are needed to transport this food globally. The greenhouse gas emissions that come partly as a result of these imported foods contribute to further climate chaos. Extreme energy mining such as hydraulic fracturing known as "fracking", along with the continued development of tar/oil sands threaten our valuable water and food sources.

The cost of food coming from far away is rising. Major climate crises such as the 2012 extreme drought in the American corn and soy belt may lead to rising food prices as most processed and packaged foods in our Canadian supermarkets include corn and soy in some form. Corn, being subsidized in the U.S., is cheap, and it is also unnaturally fed to factory-farmed animals, leading to the increase of factory-farmed meat prices. The unusual cold conditions in the southern U.S. fruit belt in 2013 and 2014 will have an impact on the availability and price of imported fruit.

Small, local farmers are more able to make flexible changes which are appropriate to local changing conditions. This is yet another reason to support local farmers who can keep on feeding us, no matter what happens elsewhere.

Eat Local to preserve diversity. Look for growers who nurture heirloom seeds and diverse varieties. The more diverse seeds that are available and suitable to a variety of conditions, the more secure our food supply is. In contrast, the one variety of tomato or carrot in our supermarket is not only boring, but also vulnerable to disaster, as were the two varieties of potato in Ireland when they were wiped out by disease. By 1845, half of the ordinary Irish people had become solely dependent on this one cheap, nourishing food. But when the potato blight struck this mono-crop, aided by an unusually wet climate, the peasant farmers had nothing else to eat and about one million Irish people died. At the same time, the gentry, mostly foreign, were growing and exporting more than enough grain to feed everyone well. Also the colonizing English had taken over the best land for raising cattle for export to England. This left only the poorest land for the Irish farmers – land that was only fit for growing potatoes. The lack of genetic variation in Irish potatoes explained why the potato blight was much more devastating in Ireland than in Europe, as the European farmers planted more diversity. This is all a lesson for our times!

> *"The loss of diversity...is a loss of divine radiance from the earth."* – Bruce Sanguin

Eat Local to strengthen local communities and family farms by keeping our food dollars in our communities. Eating local supports people who want to live with the land, take care of it, and feed us. Local farmers re-invest in local businesses, hire local labour, and contribute their civic strength to our local communities. We must resist giving our hard-earned money to faceless corporations that are worried only about the health of their bottom line, not the health of the workers, environment, and eaters. We have power in our choices.

Cheap vegetables from California (or China!) come at a hidden price. California's 1,200 major dams have so exhausted the water to grow vegetables that many rivers are almost dry by the time they reach the ocean.

"I am able to buy California lettuce year-round. I don't have to pay for the dams, the wild places given over to reservoirs and farms, and the resulting decimation of species from chinook salmon to the Least Bell's Vireo to all the plants of the bunchgrass prairies...I don't chip in on the cost of cleaning water wrecked by pesticides and herbicides used in intensive industrial farming; the health-care costs of water pollution; the greenhouse gas emissions produced in the manufacture of nitrogen-based fertilizers, which may have been shipped from the other side of the world; or the fossil fuel emissions, five times greater per mile than those from a cargo truck if the produce came to town by refrigerated jumbo jet" writes Alisa Smith in *The 100-Mile Diet.*

Eat Local to counter climate chaos, knowing that far less fossil fuel energy and fresh water is used, especially in small farm production. Think of the many energy and water efficiency strategies such as the use of smaller machinery that needs far less gas and that uses human and animal power instead; the creation of healthy soil that is able to absorb water through the use of manure from animals and plant-based fertilizers instead of synthetic chemical inputs based on fossil fuels and distant transportation. Consider the massive overall energy and water devoured in the factory-farmed meat industry.

Instead, let's protect the climate and the waters by supporting small farmers near at hand.

Eat Local to really enjoy food, knowing it is fair to farmers and animals and Earth systems. On many local family farms both animals and Nature are treated with respect and real care. Enjoy the 2011 award-winning film *To Make a Farm* by former Regina resident Steve Suderman. Compare this to the distant mega-sized industrial food system where many workers and animals live and die in cruel conditions, as shown in the 2008 film *Food Inc.*

Eat Local to teach children the wonder of food; the interlinking mystery of seeds, soil, water and air and the work of real people. Eat local to delight in real food taste as it comes in season. Eat with gratitude, respect, and joy.

Around the world, we see signs of hope. Farmers' Markets are thriving, Community Shared Agriculture (CSA) groups are spreading, front lawns are transformed with vegetables, and permaculture groups are springing up in almost every country in the world. Local citizens from Canada to Africa, from South America to India, are banding together, sometimes risking their lives, to stand up and work for their own food sovereignty on healthy land. Inventive ways of local growing are being discovered. We, the many who created this book and you the reader, are all part of this earth-sustaining, life-sustaining world-wide movement. Let's celebrate!

Chapter 4:
Bees

Bees have been honoured as sacred by Indigenous cultures around the world since early times. Bees' magical work of pollinating the flowers, gives us at least one-third of our food. Three-quarters of global food crops need insect pollination to thrive; one-third of our calories and most of our critical nutrients come from insect-pollinated crops. But now – disaster is looming! The widespread disappearance and death of honeybees is called **Colony Collapse Disorder**. Discovering and correcting the reasons is a question of survival, not only for bees, but also for us humans, their dependents.

Can we imagine a world with very little fruit or wild berries, or vegetables or nuts or seeds, or honey? What about the beauty of flowers? This is not science fiction. In the 2007 PBS Nature film *Silence of the*

Bees, scientists predict the horrifying reality: *"If the bees continue to disappear at the current rate, honeybee populations in the U.S. will cease to exist by the year 2035."*

Honey bees are the unique bees now nurtured by beekeepers in portable hives, and rented out to successive farmers to service – that is, pollinate – their crops. Since that 2007 warning, honeybees have continued to decline throughout Europe and Australia and the Americas. Other pollinators such as wild bees and butterflies are also declining.

Scientists are scrambling to discover the causes of Colony Collapse Disorder. One clear cause of the massive disappearance and death of bees appears to be **pesticide poisoning**.

Now, non-organic crops are being widely sprayed with new and more powerful neonicotinoid pesticides. France sounded the alarm when this new pesticide was introduced and their bees suddenly began to decline. Known bee symptoms of neonicotinoid poisoning are memory loss, disorientation, failure to learn and compromised immune systems. In 2013 the European Union joined many other countries in banning (for 2 years) this new culprit: pesticides containing neonicotinoids. When Italy banned them several years ago, it found that bees revived and crop production did not drop. "We don't need it!" say the farmers. In Oregon, U.S. in June 2013, 50,000 bees were found dead after neonicotinoid pesticide was used. Alas, the neonicotinoid pesticide corporations are suing the European Union for interfering with their business! Our food system has indeed gone haywire!

In Australia, 5,000 tiny sensors have been attached to bees, in an attempt to learn from their behaviour what is affecting them. In Great Britain, scientists recently announced that wild bees are found to be even more efficient pollinators than the domesticated honey bees. But now, British scientists announce that other common pesticides, pyrethroids, are found to make wild bumblebees stunted in growth and thus less efficient at foraging.

In Saskatchewan in 2013, biologist Christy Morrisey studied the effect of neonics on wetlands. She has discovered that neonics linger in wetlands at 100 times higher than the levels considered safe. Residues are also showing up in birds and insects such as bees and butterflies, our pollinators. She found that 44 percent of prairie crops are treated with neonics, as are virtually all canola crops. At the same time, prairie bees, butterflies and birds are declining in numbers.

Malnutrition is making the bees more vulnerable to all the toxic attacks from pesticides. More and more land is being turned into monoculture; especially to grow corn and canola for biofuels (food for cars - not humans). Vast monocultures leave no space for wild flowers, the necessary food for bees and other pollinators like butterflies. A worker bee (only female) flies up to three miles a day searching for suitable flowers. Bees trucked across continents in domestic hives to service crops, are often fed nutrient-deficient food such as corn syrup. Servicing a monoculture crop like blueberries or almonds, gives the bees a nutrient-deficient monoculture diet when they, like humans, need diversity. All these assaults compound the bees' problems – and ours.

Monarch butterflies and their wondrous migration share the same disappearing fate as the bees. The World Wildlife Fund reports that in the winter of 2013-14 the monarchs are occupying only 1.7 acres in Mexico, instead of 45 acres in 1996. *"The main culprit is now GMO herbicide resistant corn and soybean crops and herbicides in the USA,"* which *"leads to the wholesale killing of the monarch's principal food plant, common milkweed"* wrote entomologist Lincoln Brower. Along the monarch's flight route lies the state of Iowa. Like other grain-growing states and provinces, Iowa is covered with GM monoculture, doused with glyphosate pesticide. Iowa has lost 98% of its milkweed. In 2014 Ontario is removing common milkweed from its noxious weed list for the sake of the Monarch butterflies.

We can still change our ways, and ensure our own survival along with the bees and the butterflies by:

Switching to organic eating and growing. Organic growing along with increased field diversity nearly doubles the abundance of bees, according to the U.S. Nature Conservancy;

Rescuing, protecting and planting wild flowers and bushes which feed bees;

Switching to pesticide-free lawns, playing fields and golf courses;

Supporting smaller family farms which can nourish diversity in plants;

Being content with small blemishes on produce;

Urging our Canadian and American governments to join many other countries in banning neonicotinoid pesticides.

Honour the Bees – our Food Givers.

Learn More:

Pesticide Action Network: www.panna.org

More Than Honey. 2012 film. *"An in-depth look at honeybee colonies in California, Switzerland, China and Australia."*

Queen of the Sun: What Are the Bees Telling Us? 2010 film.

Silence of the Bees. 2007 film. PBS Nature.

A World Without Bees. Alison Benjamin and Brian McCallum. 2009

Chapter 5:
Organic or Non-Organic

"The world can feed itself with organic foods and organic farming. But if the world is subject to our western chemical agriculture system, then the cost of inputs, the energy requirements, the toxicity of the chemicals, and the degradation of the soil will be fatal." – Worldwatch Institute's State of the World 2012 report: *Nourishing the Planet*

Organic, small-farm produce is grown without any synthetic pesticides, herbicides or fertilizers. Holistic organic farming is based on caring not only for the health of eaters, but also for the health of the whole ecosystem, including the well-being of the animals, workers, communities and soil. To become a "**certified organic**" producer in Canada means that the grower has met strict regulations: the crop is grown without any chemical pesticides or fertilizers, and sold without any synthetic preservatives or additives. Organic certification is based on regular reports and yearly inspections by the government and an independent third party certifier. This certification also requires substantial payments. "Natural" or "chemical-free" is not strictly "organic," yet may or may not have met the same standards. Simply the cost deters some farmers from getting certified. In this book, "organic" is used for both "certified organic" and free of synthetic chemicals.

Produce from **organic agri-businesses** (mainly in the U.S.) is now a profitable part of the corporate food system which supplies most Canadian supermarkets. These massive businesses cannot follow the whole-earth principles of true organic growing because their focus must be the corporate aim of profit, and total separation from the eaters. However, we trust that industrial organic growers are indeed lessening the chemical loads on soil, water, climate and our bodies, which is a good thing.

Organic farming is the process of **healing the soil**, so it can provide nourishment long into the future. Soil is itself a living, breathing organism – soil is not just "dirt." *"Just one tablespoon of soil can contain up to 10 billion microbes"* writes Maria Rodale in her book *Organic Manifesto*. Synthetic pesticides and fertilizers are chemicals used in food production to kill bacteria. Pesticides are chemical or biological substances which kill living things such as insects (insecticides), plants (herbicides) and fungi (fungicides). Unfortunately, they kill *all* the bacteria. The synthetic pesticides do not know the distinction between beneficial organisms and non-beneficial organisms. **Beneficial organisms** (the good bacteria) are essential to both healthy life and healthy soil. The soil is then able to supply nutrients for healthy plants, animals and people. The good bacteria can also absorb carbon to withstand the stresses of a changing climate. Organically farmed soil has a much greater capacity to absorb moisture for the plant's use, rather than letting it run off to pollute the water.

In the magazine *Common Ground,* September 2012, author Alastair Gregor reports that

> *"Today, **systemic pesticides** are used, which cannot be washed off the food we eat. Systemic means if you spray one part of the plant, the entire plant becomes toxic and kills insects for up to 15 years; it also toxifies other organisms that eat any part of the plant and*

the fruit it produces. These toxins remain in the soil...
killing the beneficial microorganisms in the soil."

As stronger pesticides are developed the pests smartly adapt and develop into super pests so the pesticides become less effective, forcing a cycle of using more and more toxic chemicals. Also note: the nitrogen in commercial fertilizer is synthetic, and uses fossil fuel.

Glyphosate is the most commonly used broad-spectrum systemic herbicide used to kill weeds, especially annual broadleaf weeds and grasses known to compete with commercial crops grown around the globe. The main purpose of genetic modification is to protect the GM plant from the pesticide glyphosate (called RoundUp) so that the pesticide can kill everything else. This pesticide cannot be separated from the discussion on Genetically Modified Foods in Chapter 7.

Compared to conventionally grown produce, organic produce may **seem to cost more.** Organic farming demands more labour costs and also more distribution costs due to smaller quantities. Unlike conventional farming, organic farming receives no government sub-sidies. But according to the Saskatchewan Organic Directorate, if we count the value of better health and the earth's ability to provide food in the future, organic produce is far cheaper. And in the long run, as more folk buy local organic, and farmers benefit from low input costs (chemicals), the retail price will come down.

Organic production uses about **30% less fossil fuel** than chemical production, without the high fossil fuel use of large machinery and fossil-fuel based pesticides and fertilizers. Also living organic soil has much greater capacity to absorb carbon dioxide (a carbon sink), so is a real **answer to climate change.**

> *"Industrialized, globalized agriculture is a recipe for eating oil"* – Vandana Shiva

As for human health, Elizabeth Grossman's 2012 study as reported in Yale Environment 360, finds that even small doses of hormone-disrupting chemicals, found in pesticides and plastic, can interfere with the body's most vital systems. It is crucial that government "safe limits" be re-assessed.

Organic farming promotes **genetic diversity** which is essential to future food security. Organic farmers grow a variety of crops including rescuing heirloom varieties. If one fails, the diversity means that other kinds of food can fill the gap. When a huge monoculture fails, that can spell disaster. Diverse foods give diverse benefits which are lost with monoculture. Organic farmers can adjust their smaller, diverse crops to changing needs and the increasingly uncertain climate conditions.

We are left with the challenge: urge governments to assist local farmers to switch to growing organically for health of people and soil, and for food security and lower health care costs.

Something to think about: is it better to eat organic from far away, or local but chemical-laden, when these are the only options?

> *"I grow fruit organically for my own peace of mind. I know I am not hurting anyone."* – Dean Kreutzer, Over the Hill Orchards

Chapter 6:
Meat and Fish:
Free-Range and Grass-Finished or Factory-Farmed

"The conversion of Amazon Rainforest into pasture for cattle and farmland for soy crops is tantamount to taking a knife to our own lungs." – Bruce Sanguin

Whoa! Spring free of too much protein, especially meat.

The poor in many countries lack enough protein mainly because their traditional food-ways have been wholly undermined by foreign intrusion for the benefit of the "wealthy." That's us. Through mining, much of it by Canadian companies, through deforestation and agricultural pollution, through demands of the World Trade Organization and Western food we are destroying environments and ways of life which once gave nourishing food.

At the same time, people in our pampered societies are suffering from too much protein, especially meat. Kidneys are over-taxed from trying to remove excess protein and toxins from industrial meat. The high saturated fat and cholesterol in most meat can lead to heart disease and the risk of type 2 diabetes. The nitrates in most processed meat are cancer-causing if heated to high temperatures. So, eat less meat, especially hamburgers, hotdogs and ribs.

If you want to eat meat, choose it in moderation and look for **free-range** poultry, pork, lamb and grass-finished beef. Beef cattle are poor converters of grain to food protein, but they are very efficient at turning pasture grass into food protein. Grass-finished meat, compared to the common feedlot factory-farmed meat, has more protein so you can eat less of this better quality protein. Also, grass-finished meat has more Omega-3, fewer calories, less fat and far fewer toxins. It is available from some local farmers, Farmers' Markets and some Health Food stores.

Discover high-protein alternatives such as free-range chicken and eggs, fish, pulses, nuts and seeds, especially hemp seeds. Do some research on the effects of eating too much meat and visit the website www.slowfood.com.

The planet cannot sustain our modern meat-eating habits. The worldwide consumption of meat is radically increasing with the rising population and more meat diets. *"As the global population surges towards a predicted 9.1 billion people by 2050, western tastes for diets rich in meat and dairy products are unsustainable,"* says the report from United Nations Environment Program's (UNEP) international panel of sustainable resource management.

Industrial Factory-Farmed Meat and Climate Justice

"Livestock production is one of the major causes of the world's most pressing environmental problems, including global warming, land degradation, air and water pollution, and loss of biodiversity," states the 2006 report from the United Nations Food and Agriculture Organization titled *Livestock's Long Shadow: Environmental Issues and Options*.

"Lesser consumption of animal products is necessary to save the world from the worst impacts of climate change," reported the UN Environment Program in 2010.

"The life cycle and supply chain of domesticated animals raised for food account for at least half of human-caused greenhouse gases" according to the Worldwatch Institute in Nov/Dec 2009.

Feeding cattle destroys forests. 70% of former rain forests in the Amazon have been replaced by feed crops. Forests are natural carbon sinks, absorbing climate-changing carbon dioxide out of the atmosphere, as well as providing much of the world's oxygen. Another less obvious but hugely important carbon sink is organic soil. Organic soil has not been treated with chemical fertilizers and pesticides, thus protecting the soil fungi that can absorb and neutralize masses of carbon.

Commercial fertilizers and pesticides used for animal feed are made mainly with fossil fuels. Synthetic nitrogen fertilizers are high producers of the potent greenhouse gas nitrous oxide. They also rob the soil of its own nutrients, thus depriving animals so that they cannot give humans enough nutrition. Learn from Michael Pollan's book *In Defense of Food.*

Massive energy is used in feeding and watering animals. It takes 10 kilograms of grain to produce 1 kilogram of beef, 4 to 5 kilograms of grain to produce 1 kilogram of pork and 2 to 3 kilograms of grain to produce 1 kilogram of poultry.

Machines used in producing feed burn fossil fuels for energy as does transporting animals to slaughter and disposing of animal waste. Energy is also used in medical treatment of illnesses linked to poor factory-farming conditions, in processing procedures, meat refrigeration and packaging.

There are only thirteen slaughter houses in the entire U.S. Two slaughter houses process 80% of Canada's beef: Cargill and JBS Canada (formerly XL Foods) in Alberta.

Consider choosing grass-finished beef, non-medicated chicken and pork, free-range bison and lamb, sustainably harvested fish and fresh eggs from free-range chickens. Most are available year-round from some local food producers.

Industrial Factory-Farmed Meat and Animal Justice

We are not opposed to killing animals for food as it is part of Nature's way of giving and receiving, but we are opposed to suffering. We want our food to have lived with respect, and not harm the Earth.

Industrial factory-farmed meat (in most supermarkets) comes from animals raised or finished in horrific conditions. Cows are crammed into feeding lots or "concentrated animal feeding operations" (CAFO's) where they stand in their own excrement and are force-fed corn and other feed that is unnatural for cows, creating conditions in the cow's stomach that foster e-coli.

Hogs are penned together, body to body, and are not allowed to do their natural rooting and moving about. Chickens are caged and fed unnaturally to increase breast size to the point that they can barely stand up. The extreme misery of these living beings is bound to affect the health-giving quality of their meat – and our conscience!

On the other hand, cattle responsibly grass-fed on the dry, sandy prairie in south-west Saskatchewan are protecting the precious grasslands. As long as the ranchers are letting the cattle graze on the wild grasses, which need grazing since native bison are no longer doing it, the virgin land is not being dug up for various kinds of development. Then, the disappearing grassland birds, other creatures and the wild grassland flowers can survive. Only about 18% of Saskatchewan's mixed grass prairie still survives. Also, unbroken grasslands are a major carbon sink, absorbing carbon dioxide and defending the world from greater climate upheaval.

A problem for the animals, our health and the climate is that most grass-fed cattle still end up being force-fed corn in industrial feedlots before slaughter. Some ranchers avoid this by finding one of the few remaining local abattoirs and a butcher. Our beef needs to be "grass-finished" and processed through local abattoirs.

Trevor Herriot, author of *Grass, Sky, Song,* contributed the following.

> *"Beyond our personal health, there are social and environmental consequences to eating too much food that is produced high on the food chain. And yet, our grasslands need a healthy beef industry. How do we reconcile these realities? The land makes a significant energetic investment in a cow or a steer, but our economics and agricultural policy have fostered agricultural and marketing systems that do not respect that investment and instead undervalue the stewardship of our cattle-producing land and cattle-producing families. Our unwritten cheap food policy drives farm gate prices down to levels where producers find themselves participating in a process that results in unhealthy feedlot-finished meat and, sometimes, damaged landscapes and reduced grassland biodiversity. Beef consumption has been much higher on a per capita level than it was prior to World War II. If we were to eat beef but at the same time pay beef producers more per pound of healthy, grass-finished beef raised in ecologically sustainable conditions, keeping some beef in our diets would become an unassailable way to sustain the environment and stay healthy. If we paid properly for the stewardship it takes to produce beef sustainably, it would help conserve the ranching culture that has held onto some of our native grasslands despite the pressures of an increasingly industrialized and consolidated meat processing system run by three large corporations. Heading the other direction, we are losing our traditional, ranching stewardship*

culture, and the burrowing owls and many other grassland creatures, spirit made flesh, who depend on well-managed native grassland."

Industrial Factory-Farmed Meat and Human Health

Antibiotics are intended only to combat sickness. But industrial factory-farmed animals are all pumped with antibiotics to combat unhealthy conditions and to increase growth. So we factory-farmed meat-eaters become less protected by antibiotics because we have absorbed too much of them. The World Health Organization reports that one of the biggest threats to human health today is antibiotic resistance, stating *"It is estimated that the use of antibiotics in farm animals and fish is almost a thousandfold that of human use."* Reports are available about the new global epidemic, the C. difficile infection, born of too much antibiotic use.

Most local, small-farm animals are raised with respect and in as natural conditions as possible. It is ideal if the animals are grass-fed and better still grass-finished, as Nature intended. Their meat certainly tastes better, is more filling, far more nutritious and free from chemicals such as unnecessary antibiotics. So small-farm meat is bound to give us more health. If it costs a little more, eat less meat and increase your consumption of beans, which are cheap.

Bison is truly Canadian meat. Its ancestors were not imported from other lands. Nutritionally, bison beats beef. Bison is totally grass-fed and given no growth hormones, steroids or antibiotics. Bison has 40% more protein than beef, 1/3 less fat and fewer calories, but is loaded with other nutrients, especially iron and selenium. Bison cooks faster than beef and is delicious.

Fish

> *"Quit beefing—eat fish"* – sign in a fish shop

Local fish was a revered staple of our ancestors, and still is today for many Indigenous people. Fish is an excellent protein alternative to meat and gives special nutrients. Fish is rich in Omega-3 fatty acids, vitamin D and selenium. Fish aids the health of eyes, heart, nervous system and brain development.

Salmon: Wild or Farmed? Or local fish?

Most salmon available in our supermarkets and restaurants are open net Atlantic salmon farmed on the west coast. In this method, fish are cramped in pens that are open to the ocean. Their waste and their pesticides and antibiotics can pollute the ocean waters and wild fish. Also the Atlantic **farmed salmon** can escape to contaminate the wild Pacific salmon, which are a different species. Fortunately, some fish farms, even in Alberta, are now "closed containment", a new technology welcomed by the David Suzuki Foundation. The Namgis First Nation Closed Containment Salmon Farm in B.C. is the first company in North America to grow closed containment Atlantic salmon on a commercial scale. But another problem with farmed salmon is their feed; it takes four kilos of small fish to make one kilo of feed for farmed salmon, using a mass of energy to make the pellets. These small fish usually come from the coasts of South America, thus are stolen from local food sources.

Compared to **wild Pacific salmon**, farmed salmon are far higher in fat, which accumulates more toxins including cancer-causing PCB's. Compared to wild salmon, farmed salmon have less protein and far lower levels of vitamins D and A.

While Aboriginal groups fish wild Pacific salmon respectfully in B.C. under very strict regulations, wild Pacific salmon is over-fished by others, and stressed by climate change and development. Canned pink salmon is wild, not farmed.

It seems better to eat similar steelhead trout from Saskatchewan's Lake Diefenbaker, although it too is farmed, and connected to a waterway, the South Saskatchewan River. We need to know more. Some folk think steelhead is even tastier and more delicate than salmon! Also if we live in Saskatchewan, let's explore the good local fish from Saskatchewan's northern waters and support our northern fisher folk; Saskatchewan fish include steelhead trout (farmed), northern pike, whitefish, and pickerel (walleye). Or find the fish local to where you live.

Farming shrimp also brings problems. Huge coastal shrimp pens keep the local fisher folk in South America and Asia away from their coast and water space, and keep fish away from the fishers' nets. In *Stolen Harvest,* Vandana Shiva reports that in India *"shrimp cultivation destroys 15 jobs for each job it creates. For every acre of an industrial shrimp farm, 200 acres of productive ecosystems are destroyed.... Salt water from the shrimp pens seeps into farmers' soil and groundwater. Shrimp farms destroy mangroves which play a crucial ecological role in coastal ecosystems, protecting against tropical storms (tsunamis), providing habitat for fish and other marine life."* Mangroves top even rain forests in absorbing climate-changing carbon dioxide. Rodale News reports that in the last 50 years, in the leading shrimp-farming countries such as Thailand, Ecuador, Indonesia, China, Mexico and Vietnam, up to 80% of the mangroves have been destroyed to make way for more shrimp farms. United Nations agencies call shrimp farms "rape and run" industries because they soon fail, having done their devastation.

Shrimp also carry severe health problems for the eaters. Most farmed shrimp is loaded with a range of antibiotics and pesticides to combat the pathogens due to their unhealthy living conditions. The fish meal fed to farmed shrimp also carries chemical contaminants, such as dioxin and PCBs which can lead to hormone disruption, immune system disorders and cancer in the human shrimp eaters.

Let's demand that farmed salmon and shrimp be produced in sustainable ways, with tough inspections. But more importantly, eat less. *"As long as shrimp demand is not reduced, the industry will continue to be out of control"* even if better standards are achieved, said Alfredo Quarto of the Mangrove Action Project.

But alas, we are advised to eat fish no more than twice a week because of mercury and other pollutants. What about the northern people who depend on fish for their nourishment?

Our best seafood choices, according to David Suzuki, are the little fish: sardines, anchovies, herring and mackerel. The lower on the food chain, the less ecosystem energy is needed to sustain them. Also these little fish are cheap food, and hold a wealth of nutrients.

Here is David Suzuki's list of Sustainable Seafood that is harvested in a way that protects the ocean ecosystems: swordfish caught by harpoon or handline (contains high mercury levels); sardines; albacore tuna (low mercury); Pacific cod, caught in Alaskan waters; farmed clams and oysters; closed containment farmed salmon; and wild salmon caught in Alaskan waters.

Brunswick (Black's Harbour, NB) is North America's only producer of canned sardines, and the world's largest. It is also a good company to work for.

Saskatchewan Co-ops are partnering with *Sea Choice*, the conservation coalition that rates fish on an eco-scale. Visit SeaChoice.org.

Chapter 7:
Genetically Modified Foods

"Genetic modification threatens to unbalance the biosphere, create 'super-weeds', endanger beneficial insects, and erode bio-diversity. Bio-diversity is a vital source of raw materials for agriculture and an essential component of environmental well-being."

– National Farmers' Union

Genetic Modification (GM) is the insertion of genes from one distinct organism into the genome of a totally different organism. The result is called a Genetically Modified Organism or GMO. Genetic modification is not like traditional hybridization and selective breeding as practiced by farmers since agriculture began. Working with Nature, those farmers developed hundreds of varieties of seeds by patient selection. By contrast, GM can include inserting a fish gene into a tomato so it will pack and travel better.

Most GM seeds are owned by biotech giants and modified to withstand the biotech pesticide Glyphosate (RoundUp). RoundUp is designed to kill most non-modified plants, which in turn results in the loss of beneficial insects, and wild flowers which are essential for bees and butterflies – our pollinators. Only plants grown from GM seeds are spared.

Because some weeds have developed into super resistant weeds, GM crops require more and more pesticide and the result is ever increasing costs for the farmers, who every year have to keep paying rising prices for the seeds and pesticides.

Almost all Saskatchewan-grown canola and soybeans are GMO. Because wind spreads the pollen, GM crops contaminate surrounding organic crops. Organic wheat, alfalfa and flax are also threatened if the GM versions of their seeds are allowed into Canada. So far, Canadian wheat farmers have been successful in their struggle to keep GM wheat out of Canada, as Emily Eaton recounts in her 2013 book: *Growing Resistance: Canadian Farmers and the Politics of Genetically Modified Wheat.*

Genetic Modification has devastating effects. Here are 6 of them:

1. GM **unbalances the biosphere**, creating super-weeds and destroying habitat and genetic diversity. Once genetically modified organisms are released into our environment they cannot be controlled or recalled.

2. Chemical pesticides **weaken a plant's healthy growth systems and natural defenses** because the chemicals do the defending for them. As a result, GM plants treated by Glyphosate have a weaker ability to nourish both animal and human eaters. Studies have shown Glyphosate fields that are unable to withstand severe drought, while GMO-free fields adapt and survive. Glyphosate is also blamed for an epidemic of animal sickness and death in the U.S. and South Africa where they are fed GM corn. The animals' digestive systems do not know how to use GM corn as food.

3. Even worse, Glyphosate **threatens the future**. It contains a surfactant, which enables the pesticide to get right into the cellular structure of the plant, not just onto the surface, and then through the roots into the soil. There this toxin stays for years, ready to affect future crops.

4. The use of Genetic Modification imposes foreign **corporate control** over farmers, who experience ever-increasing costs for patented seeds and pesticides, while making huge profits for biotech corporations. Farmers are forbidden to save their seeds and replant them in the traditional way. The result is the destruction of traditional food growing cultures in Canada and around the world. In India, every half-hour, one farmer commits suicide because of these pressures from foreign seed and pesticide companies. Vandana Shiva says in the film Bitter Seeds *"This enormous pressure of [biotech giants] on governments across the world is a major threat to the future of seeds, the future of food, and the future of democracy."* Shiva is a world-renowned environmental thinker, activist and author, formerly India's leading physicist.

5. GM brings **Food Insecurity.** *"Industrial agriculture has not produced more food. It has destroyed diverse sources of food, using huge quantities of fossil fuels and water and toxic chemicals in the process"* says Vandana Shiva, in *Stolen Harvest.*

   "Genetic Engineering is not about feeding the world. It is about feeding the companies that are the promoters of GMO," says Marc Loiselle, farmer in the Saskatchewan Organic Directorate.

6. There have been no systematic, scientific studies of **human health effects** of eating GM foods. However, separate studies have indicated a probable link between GMO/Glyphosate-treated food and a multitude of human illnesses, of which many are now epidemics such as: Alzheimer's, Autism, Asthma, Cancer, Crohn's Disease, Obesity and Birth Defects. Moreover, a 2012 study reported by the Canadian School of Natural Nutrition reveals that medical patients who followed strict GMO-free diets experienced dramatic health improvement. The only way to avoid GMOs is to avoid most processed food because *"Nearly 80% of non-organic processed foods and meats contain GMO/ Glyphosate-treated ingredients, especially forms of corn and*

soy" says Jeffrey Smith in *Genetic Roulette.*

"Because fertilizers, chemicals, and other technologies failed to fulfill their promises of farm profitability, many farmers rightly question the economic benefits of genetically modifying crops and livestock.... Further, the proliferation of some GM crops has effectively deprived many organic farmers of the option to grow those crops....More than any other technology... patented seeds sold through contract...clearly erode farmers' autonomy....Because this technology has the potential to threaten the environment, human health, and the economic wellbeing of farmers, Canadians should debate and study before we plant and eat." – The National Farmers' Union Policy on Genetically Modified Foods.

GM CROPS GROWN IN CANADA		
CROP	**TRAIT**	**WHERE ON THE SHELVES**
CORN	Insect resistant, herbicide tolerant	Corn flakes; Corn chips; Cornstarch; Corn syrup; Corn oil and other corn ingredients in processed foods; Sweeteners like glucose and fructose; Eggs, milk and meat; Some sweetcorn
CANOLA	Herbicide tolerant	Canola oil; Eggs, milk and meat
SOY	Herbicide tolerant	Soy oil; Soy protein; Soy lecithin; Tofu; Soy beverages; Soy puddings; Eggs, milk and meat
SUGAR BEET	Herbicide tolerant	Sugar
Reprinted with permission from CBAN. www.cban.ca/gmfoods		

GM FOODS IMPORTED TO CANADA		
FOOD	**GROWN**	**WHERE ON THE SHELVES**
COTTONSEED OIL	U.S.	Cottonseed oil; Vegetable oil in processed foods such as potato chips
PAPAYA	U.S. (Hawaii)	Papaya in fruit juices and other processed foods
SQUASH	U.S.	Some zucchini; Yellow crookneck and straighneck squash
MILK PRODUCTS (BOVINE GROWTH HORMONE)	U.S.	Milk solids and powder; Frozen desserts with dairy; Imported mixed drinks with milk ingredients
Reprinted with permission from CBAN. www.cban.ca/gmfoods		

Learn More:

Much of the Glyphosate information here is based on *"Failed Promises, Flawed Science: Impact of Glyphosate & GMO Contamination on Crop, Animal and Human Health,"* a lecture by Dr. Don Huber, Professor Emeritus, Purdue University. Organic Connections Conference. Regina, SK. November 1, 2012.

BillMoyers.com

Canadian Biotechnology Action Network (CBAN) at www.cban.ca.

Genetic Roulette: The Gamble of our Lives. Jeffrey M. Smith. 2012.

Genetically Modified Crops: Promises, Perils, and the Need for Public Policy, Quaker Institute for the Future, 2011. On-line at www.quaker-institute.org.

GM Fails To Raise Crop Yields, International Study Finds, John Vidal. CCPA Monitor, February 2012.

GM Seed Threat. Vandana Shiva. CCPA Monitor, May 2012.

Hijacked Future: Who Controls the Seed Controls our Food. Dir. David Springbett. Canada. 2008.

National Farmers' Union. Policy on Genetically Modified Foods. www.nfu.ca.

www.nongmoproject.org

www.nongmoshoppingguide.com

Organic Manifesto: How Organic Farming Can Heal Our Planet, Feed the World and Keep Us Safe. Maria Rodale. 2010.

www.responsibletechnology.org

Stolen Harvest: The Hijacking of the Global Food Supply. Vandana Shiva. 2000.

Chapter 8:
Plastics and BPA

The Problem with Tin Cans: BPA

Many foods are sold in cans lined with the plastic BPA (Bisphenol A), which is an endocrine disrupter that interferes with hormones in the body. BPA is linked to diabetes, cancer, ADHD, heart disease, infertility issues and neurological behavioural problems, even in babies fed on canned food. Animal research links BPA to aggressive behaviour, early sexual maturity and developmental problems. BPA especially can leach into acidic, salty and fatty foods that are canned such as tomatoes, soup, vegetables and coconut oil. BPS (Bisphenol S) is touted by some companies as a substitute for BPA in can linings, but so far it seems to have similar worrying effects as BPA. So, let's avoid canned food and discover the satisfaction of "starting from scratch."

Plastic Containers, Wrap and Bottles

Plastic containers should never be used when thawing frozen food or preparing hot food. Toxic chemicals from the plastic can leach into the food. Never use plastic in a microwave as this releases some of the chemical building blocks in plastic, and leaches them into the food or drink.

The **microwave oven** itself is problematic. Microwave ovens are considered to change the molecular structure of food, destroy vitamin A and some other vitamins, convert some amino acids or alkaloids into carcinogens, and lead to other health problems. Although microwave ovens are convenient and energy efficient, it is best to use a toaster oven or stove to heat up food. Of course, there are differing opinions about microwave ovens and the use of "microwave-safe plastic"; is it safe for the humans or just for the plastic? So do your own research, then do what you can in your situation.

Plastic water bottles pollute landfills, water tables and Earth. They have to be manufactured, filled, transported and recycled, devouring fossil fuels along the way. Plastic water bottles are usually #3 PUC, which is dangerous for our health and known to leach endocrine and hormone disrupting chemicals, even more so the longer the water sits in the plastic. Plastic bottles take 450 years to break down and plastic bags take up to 1,000 years. Many of our plastic shopping and food storage bags end up in the lakes or oceans where water creatures such as sea turtles ingest them and die.

Guide to Food-Storing Plastics

#1 PET (Polyethylene Terephthalate) is in many water and pop bottles and also in some food jars and muffin containers. Although these containers are considered relatively safe for food, the longer food is left in them, the more leaching is likely. Using these containers more than once increases the risk of leaching carcinogens into the contents. Workers employed in the manufacture of this plastic are exposed to toxins causing serious health problems.

#2 HDPE (High-density Polyethylene) is the most resistant to chemical leaching. It is used in milk jugs, water and juice containers, opaque plastic bags as well as yogurt and similar tubs. This plastic is never see-through.

#3 PVC (Polyvinyl Chloride) is known to leach toxins that are considered endocrine and hormone disrupters, mimicking the female hormone estrogen. PVC is linked to childhood allergies and asthma, and possibly to cancer and other health effects. It is even dubbed "the poison plastic" because it contains numerous toxins that can leach into food and beverages. PVC is most common in drinking water bottles, baby bottles, cooking oil bottles and plastic food wrapping. Try to avoid and never re-use.

#4 LDPE (Low Density Polyethylene) is used in sandwich bags, bread bags, plastic grocery bags and squeezable bottles. LDPE is considered "less toxic" than other plastics.

#5 PP (Polypropylene) is used in syrup bottles and yogurt containers, potato chip bags, straws and cereal box liners. PP is considered safe for re-use.

#6 PS (Polystyrene) is Styrofoam. It is used for disposable coffee cups and take-out containers. PS is known to leach styrene, a human carcinogen. PS chemicals are linked with reproductive system and human health issues. PS is also a planet-wide hazard because it breaks into smaller bits and blows into our lakes and oceans and poisons water life.

#7 PC (Other plastics) is the worst. It is no longer found in baby bottles, but may be found in reusable water bottles and 5 gallon jugs. PC sometimes contains BPA.

We do the best we can by using glass, steel, cloth and paper for food storage as much as possible. Then **we eat lots of food with antioxidants to clean up the toxins we can't avoid.**

Chapter 9:
Food Demystified

"To know what you're eating, is the beginning of food sovereignty." – Nettie Wiebe

Beverages

Tap Water or Bottled Water?

Plain water is Nature's best gift, the life-blood of Mother Earth. Tap into it, unless you are in a community where, to our shame, tap water is not safe. How many Aboriginal communities in your province cannot drink their water?

Good tap water is the best thirst-quencher, but some feel that filtered reverse osmosis tap water is better still. Let tap water sit open in a glass pitcher or jar for 8 hours, while much of the chlorine evaporates. Carry it in a steel or glass container, not plastic. You can add a few mint or basil leaves or a squeeze of lemon.

Tap water is just as safe as, and probably safer than bottled water, because bottled water is usually less regulated than municipal water systems. About 40% of bottled water sold in Canada is tap water that is processed through filtration and reverse osmosis to kill bacteria. The rest is pumped from underground springs, with corporations paying little or nothing for it, and then selling for vastly magnified prices.

In developing countries such as India and Pakistan, huge bottled water corporations are draining the aquifers. Groundwater levels are plunging. Families deprived of water to grow their food, are driven into poverty and despair and whole areas are made uninhabitable. Also, plastic water bottles are a major problem for the planet and for the drinkers' health. **See Chapter 8: Plastics**. These same issues apply to water used for the production of pop.

Let's support our publicly-owned water systems rather than giant multinational corporations.

Pop

Give POP a pass! Soft drinks or "liquid candy" are made of a mix of phosphoric acid (the fizz), sugar, caffeine, colouring, and artificial flavouring. High phosphorous pulls calcium out of the bones, which can lead to osteoporosis and broken bones; girls especially beware! Some soft drinks have almost as much caffeine as does coffee. Soft drinks' sugar and acid dissolve teeth, especially for children. Soft drinks can decrease the body's iron and decrease the effects of penicillin. Sugar gives a feast to cancer cells, and pop is a major cause of the obesity epidemic. Major pop giants over-exploit and pollute water resources in India, Ghana, Mexico and other countries. Production of soft drinks requires a vast amount of fossil fuel.

Diet pop is no healthier. Drinking one or more soft drinks a day, no matter if diet or regular, can lead up to a 30 percent greater chance of weight gain. Diet pop contains artificial sweeteners which are possibly dangerous, as well as other questionable additives. Studies show that when people drink diet pop they are likely to eat more.

Also consider that most pop cans are lined with the endocrine disruptor BPA. "Vitaminized water" may be a source of sugar.

Fruit Juice

Studies find that fruit juice spikes blood sugar the same as pop does. Even 100% fruit juice with no sugar added has as much sugar as pop. This is because the natural sugar in fresh fruit is so concentrated in juice without the fruit's fibre to slow down sugar absorption. The Harvard Gazette (August 2013) reported a study that found that eating 2 servings a week of whole fruit such as blueberries or apples resulted in a 23% reduced risk of type 2 diabetes; but a daily serving of fruit juice resulted in a 21% increase in type 2 diabetes risk. Dentists warn that in fruit juice high acid combined with high sugar wears down the calcium in young teeth, so should not be in a baby's bottle. The process of concentrating the juice takes out most of the nutrients, so let's eat whole fruit. If you must have fruit juice, water it down.

Milk

Milk brings a bundle of benefits, but some concerns for some people. **See Chapter 9: Fat, Milk Eggs.**

Tea

Dandelion Tea is my morning tonic – a handful of dandelion leaves, washed, with a bit of mint – every morning from the first radiant flower until the last leaves before the snow. As the older leaves are picked at the base, new tender leaves grow. So gather Nature's golden gift of health, with thanks! Steep the leaves in not-quite-boiling water for 15 minutes. Goes well combined with mint. It is a diuretic, among a host of other health bonuses, so don't drink at bedtime! **See Chapter 9: Vegetables** for more benefits.

Green Tea has many disease-fighting properties, due to its high flavonoid content (antioxidants derived from plants). So green tea gives benefits such as halting damage to cells, reducing risk of cancer and heart disease.

Mint, lemon balm and other local herbs make refreshing and healing teas.

Prairie Tea catches the goodness in berries of the prairies, especially saskatoons. You can find it at specialty shops.

Rooibos Tea (roy-boss) meaning "red bush," organic, Fair Trade, from South Africa is a healthy alternative to daily coffee. Like Green tea, rooibos gives antioxidant action against bad free radicals. Rooibos is caffeine-free, rich in minerals, and can be used for heart health. Rooibos eases nervous tension, blood pressure, headaches, insomnia, allergies, liver, respiratory and digestive problems, fights cancer, boosts the immune system and more. Worth a try! You can add a bit of honey – or not.

Yerba Mate is a wild shrub from Argentina, traditionally used for its many health benefits.

Coffee

Fair Trade and organic coffee is grown in the traditional way, under a forest canopy, using natural methods, not toxic chemicals to deal with pests. Coffee grown this way protects the workers, and provides habitat for "our" Migratory Birds like the Baltimore Oriole, Scarlet Tanager and Wood Thrush. Most regular coffee now is grown in full sun in deforested areas, needing many chemical inputs, leading to more misery for workers and no refuge for our endangered birds, according to the Canadian Wildlife Federation.

> *When eating fruit, remember who planted the tree; when drinking clear water, remember who dug the well.* – Vietnamese proverb

Fat, Milk, Eggs

Fat

> *"Consider the gift of fat."* – Sandra Brandt

When you buy oil, think about: "Where did it come from? ... How was it produced? ... What are its health benefits or dangers?"

Camelina oil for Canadian use was first developed in Saskatchewan when local farmers began processing locally grown camelina. Camelina grows easily in prairie conditions and has been traditionally cultivated as an oilseed crop in Europe for at least 3,000 years. Now, a Manitoba company, Fairfield Organics, is producing camelina oil which is certified organic and therefore non-GMO. The Saskatchewan Three Farmers oil is certified non-GMO (but is not organic). Camelina oil is very high in vitamin E, antioxidants and Omega-3 essential fatty acids. It is cold-pressed; has a long shelf life so resists becoming rancid, and is found in specialty stores.

Canola oil is produced in Saskatchewan, but here it is probably 100% GMO, contributing to soil and ecosystem deterioration, with worrying health effects (as explained in Chapter 7). The film *How Canola Is Made* shows some of the problems.

Coconut oil is mostly from destructive monoculture plantations. But some, available in our Health Food stores, is produced on small Fair Trade farms in the Philippines. Organic virgin coconut oil is extremely high in good saturated fat, a rich source of Omega-3 with many other health benefits.

Extra Virgin Olive oil travels far (most from Italy), but may be best for our health. **Zatoun** olive oil is certified Fair Trade, usually organic, and is made by Palestinian farmers from their own olive trees, bottled in glass, not plastic (www.zatoun.com). Olive oil is the only oil that can be eaten just as is, freshly pressed from the fruit. Extra virgin is best, because it is less processed. It is high in "good" unsaturated fatty acids and antioxidants, particularly vitamin E. Some olive oil is organic. Olive oil should be stored in a cool, dark place, and kept airtight.

Flax seed oil is high in Omega-3 and has other mighty nutrients, but has a short shelf life.

Palm oil comes from huge palm tree plantations that displace the forest, the wildlife and the forest-dwelling peoples, with its destructive monoculture. Palm oil is a major cause of climate upheaval, because the plantations raze huge tracts of rainforest, which are among the world's largest carbon sinks and oxygen producers. Palm oil is in about half of the products on supermarket shelves, often camouflaged as "vegetable oil" as reported by the *Rainforest Action Network*.

Butter or Margarine?

Just look at what is in them! Margarine is made of man-made fat engineered to become highly processed hydrogenated vegetable oil. Some even have trans-fat, with many additives including colouring dye. Margarine gives Omega-6 fatty acid of which we have too much.

Butter has 30% monounsaturated fat, the good kind that is the same as in olive oil, nuts, avocados and fatty fish. Butter's colour is from natural carotene, giving vitamin A. Butter is also a good source of Omega-3 and other needed nutrients. Omega-3 helps build a strong immune system and supports the health of brain, heart, liver, lungs, and nervous system. Butter fat and other saturated fats help the body absorb nutrients such as Omega-3 and calcium from other foods. As people stopped eating lard, butter and other animal fat, and started eating more sugar laden food, heart attacks increased, reported Michael Pollan in his 2009 book *In Defense of Food.*

Better Butter Recipe (stays soft)

1 cup (250 mL) butter (1/2 brick)
2/3 cup (150 mL) camelina oil or extra virgin olive oil

Leave butter at room temperature until soft and slice into small cubes. In blender, whiz together butter and oil until smooth. Refrigerate.

Milk

Milk (Dairy)

It is best to buy organic dairy foods if possible. This is because of the prevalent use of antibiotics in the cows to increase milk production and control infections, and the antibiotics are passed into the milk products.

Cheese

The orange colour in cheese (unlike many other synthetic "food" dyes) is really natural, from the seeds of the Achiote tree. Saskatchewan farmers are making various cheeses, such as delicious and healthy goat cheese (to make a dip add some plain yogurt). Goat milk and goat cheese are easier to digest. Compared to cows' cheddar, goat cheese has less lactose and salt, fewer harmful additives like antibiotics, but similar nutrients.

Beware of processed cheap, unhealthy cheese inserted into a host of processed "foods."

Natural yogurt

Yogurt is a wonder-working food, cherished in the Middle East for maybe 2,000 years. Natural probiotic yogurt contains the beneficial living bacteria which do the good work in our intestines, helping with digestion, making our colon healthy, stimulating immunity and killing bad germs. Yogurt is especially important to eat after completing antibiotics, to replenish the friendly bacteria from the depleting, harming effects of the antibiotics in the intestine. Yogurt must be eaten regularly to maintain the digestive benefits.

Yogurt is rich in calcium that works with the live cultures to increase absorption in the bones. Yogurt is a calcium boon for people who are lactose-intolerant because it contains lactase, the enzyme which breaks down lactose in milk for proper digestion. Yogurt is rich in protein as well as calcium, B vitamins and essential minerals.

Homemade Yogurt

A candy thermometer is handy.

Take 4 cups (1 L) milk (2%, whole or powdered mixed with water. Powdered milk is cheaper but not as healthy because it lacks the nutritious butter fat).

And 1/3 cup (75 mL) store-bought plain yogurt, with active bacterial cultures (first time only; later, use your own home-made yogurt as starter).

Take the starter yogurt out of the fridge so it can warm to room temperature.

Heat the milk in a saucepan on medium heat, stirring often, until it reaches 180°F (85°C) or when tiny bubbles appear (to kill the bacteria which might interfere with the process). Then let cool to 110°F (45°C) or until you can hold a finger in it for 10 seconds. To hurry the cooling, pour milk into a bowl and set inside a larger bowl of cold water.

When the milk is the right temperature, add the plain yogurt and stir well.

Pour the mixture into two wide-mouth thermos bottles (warm them first with hot water, this makes a difference!). Let it sit for about 8 hours or more at room temperature. Then refrigerate the yogurt while still in the thermos, but replace the lid with a thin cover, such as wax paper to allow it to cool.

OR – Pour the mixture into glass jars with lids. Set in a large pot of warm water and cover. Set on a heating pad at medium temperature.

Wrap with a towel and let sit 6 or more hours. Letting it sit longer increases thickening.

OR – place jars in oven set at the pilot light or lowest possible temperature; turn heat off before it gets too hot. Let sit 6 or more hours. Letting it sit longer increases thickening.

Use this yogurt to start the next batch, so there is no need to buy more. It is a good idea to save 1/3 cup (75 mL) of the new batch in a small jar so it doesn't get eaten. Use starter within 5 to 7 days, before it loses its fermenting power.

If the yogurt doesn't set, add more starter and try again.

By making your own yogurt, you can use the kind of milk you want. Homemade yogurt is not stored in health-questionable plastic, and you can avoid wasting plastic containers (consolidated fossil fuel), and is less costly to the environment and to your wallet.

Yogurt cream cheese and whey: whey is the liquid sometimes on top of commercial yogurt or remaining after yogurt has been curdled and strained. To make whey and yogurt cream cheese: place some yogurt in a square of clean white cloth (cheesecloth or other fine cloth), tie a string around it, then hang up to drip into a bowl underneath. That clear liquid is whey. Remaining inside the cloth is a lovely cream cheese.

Whey: naturally inoculates foods from bad bacteria, so that good bacteria can do their work. Whey protein is complete protein, containing all 9 essential amino acids and is easily digested. Whey contains low levels of fat and lactose. The whey can be used in baking, smoothies and soup, in cooking rice or other grains or in making sauerkraut. Whey keeps in the fridge up to 6 months.

Greek Yogurt is strained, removing the liquid whey, making it thicker and creamier, with double the protein yet half the salt.

Flavoured yogurt is so popular and handy, but it has additives: usually lots of sugar along with the fruit, probably dye, preservatives, less real milk and no living culture. Avoid "low-fat" labels as butterfat contains vital nutrients and digestion aids.

Alternatives to Cow's Milk

Goat Milk is considered close to a perfect food. It is recommended by most naturopaths as a substitute for cow's milk because it is low on the allergy scale. Goat milk is non-mucous-forming.

As an alternative to cow's milk, **hemp beverage** is preferable because it is prairie local, organic and non-GMO, having the super health benefits of hemp seeds. Hemp Bliss is produced by Manitoba Harvest, a large farmer-owned hemp food manufacturing company. It comes in several flavours and the plain unsweetened variety works well in soups and baking.

Soy or almond "milk", unless organic, are both GMO. Almonds in almond drink, unless organic, are heavily sprayed and so a major contributor to the death of bees. Rice in rice "milk" comes from far away and usually requires much water in growing (although a new System of Rice Intensification uses far less water).

The best **non-dairy sources of calcium** are sesame seeds, tahini (sesame butter), almonds, figs, broccoli, raw spinach, Swiss Chard, kale and other dark green leafy vegetables (especially dandelions!). Also lima and navy beans, carrots, raisins, dates, oranges, millet and oats, red raspberry leaf tea, arrowroot (use the powder instead of cornstarch for thickening), blackstrap molasses and kelp.

Eggs

One-a-Day is A-O.K. and now the whole egg is good for us! Current USDA studies show that eggs have less cholesterol and more vitamins than formerly thought, so there are no connections between eating eggs and heart disease and stroke. Whole eggs are a super source of protein, vitamin A, minerals, and essential vitamin D. They are low in saturated fat and calories. So now we can enjoy this alternative to meat, in moderation, with a clear conscience.

A free-range egg has a darker yolk, thanks to the extra beta-carotene and other nutrients from the fresh clover and grass the happy hens enjoyed. Free-range hens are given many hours of freedom to live the natural lives of hens, and are moved about to eat grass and provide manure for different parts of the farm. However, corporate eggs labelled "free-range" might be from hens allowed only a token time-out, perhaps only in a barn, not on grass. Small-farm eggs labelled "free-range" are not necessarily fed organic feed but at least compared to "caged eggs" they have less fat, four times more vitamin D, seven times more vitamin A, three times more vitamin E, and many times more Omega-3 fatty acid. Eggs labelled "Omega-3" are from caged hens fed flax to raise their eggs' Omega-3 level to that of true free-range eggs. Small-farm eggs labelled "organic" are from hens that have been given free range; also they are fed organic feed, thus taking care of the soil and the hens in their whole life cycle.

Fruit

Gathering

*Saskatoons glowing fuchsia red to midnight blue
joyous gift from three-year lack.
I reach out and receive giving thanks to
berry bush and birdsong
earth's mystic synchronicity of sun and rain
and power to give in myriad forms.
Watching out for ivy's poison
guarding berries safe for birds
not greedy humans.
I reach out and receive.*

*I take, remembering
remembering my sisters
in this prairie valley, the Qu'Appelle
Cree, Assinaboia and Métis
since time immemorial honouring Earth's cycles
planning, gathering, sharing the gifts
Saskatoons glowing fuchsia to midnight blue.
They reached out and received,
giving thanks.
I too, remembering.*

Catherine Verrall, August 2008, Lumsden Beach, Saskatchewan.
*"Again in 2012, there were few wild saskatoon berries in the
Qu'Appelle Valley. Spring had come far too soon, tricking the
blossoms, then followed winter frost. We humans are upsetting
Nature's exquisite synchronicity with climate upheaval."*

Apples top the healthiest-of-all fruits list, if they are organic. The skin provides fibre and apples give a heaping dose of flavonoid antioxidants, which reduce the risk of heart disease, stroke and cancer. Local apples even if imperfect can be stewed, skin on, cores removed, to make winter applesauce, perked with cinnamon, ginger, nutmeg, fennel or cardamom. Or mix with cranberry or rhubarb sauce. Organic Canadian apples from B.C. can be bought all winter.

Apricots are loaded with good stuff, especially beta carotene (vitamin A) which protects eyes, helps prevent cancer and maintains a healthy immune system. Apricots also give vitamin C, calcium, and heart-healthy potassium.

Berries: Saskatchewan is rich in cultivated fruit, although much of our former riches in wild berries as a health source for Aboriginal people and early settlers are being destroyed by careless development and monoculture. Besides being delicious treats, berries carry a host of benefits. Berries are very high in powerful antioxidants including vitamin C. **Haskap berries** were developed by the University of Saskatchewan Fruit Program – large, tart, juicy, blue-coloured berries similar in taste to blueberries.

Blueberries and **saskatoon berries** top the antioxidant benefits list and also help prevent high blood pressure, macular degeneration and brain damage. A recent study shows that berries keep our brains sharp. At Brigham and Women's Hospital, Boston, senior women whose diet included a high intake of berries such as blueberries and strawberries, could delay memory decline by 2-5 years. For winter, berries freeze beautifully, with no sugar. Rinse, place in a single layer on a tray, freeze until hard, then pack quickly into glass jars or freezer bags.

Cherries are very high in iron and disease-fighting flavonoids, as well as potassium, magnesium, vitamins C, E and heart-protecting carotenoids. Cherries reduce inflammation, arthritic and gout pain, and cancer risk. For winter, cherries freeze beautifully, with no sugar. Rinse, squeeze out the pit, place in a single layer on a tray, and freeze until hard, pack quickly into freezer bags or glass jars leaving 1/2 inch headspace. Frozen, organic, pitted cherries are available all year.

Cranberries are so effective in healing, that both Western medicine and Natural Health doctors rely on their powers – especially for healing urinary tract and eye disorders, as well as a host of other problems. Don't wait for Christmas! Let raw or frozen cranberries perk up pancakes, baking, soup and smoothies, all year round. Serve homemade cranberry sauce with any meat, fish, egg or vegetarian dish; stir into a salad or applesauce. *To cook cranberries:* stew raw cranberries briefly and add a bit of local honey but keep the zing! The less fruit is cooked, the more benefits it has as less vitamin C is destroyed. Saskatchewan's wild high-bush cranberries make wonderful jam or juice.

To make high-bush cranberry juice, heat cranberries in water to just under boiling, enough to loosen the pits without destroying the vitamin C. Then smash them and put them in a blender for a momentary whiz; press through a sieve to remove the pits and skin. To drink it needs little, if any, honey.

Rhubarb is technically a vegetable, but we use it like a fruit. Rhubarb is rich in vitamin C, A, K and fibre. Rhubarb acts as a natural laxative and detoxifier, is great for diabetes, cardiovascular disease and may give medicinal help in a variety of other conditions. Note that the leaves are toxic so put them in the garbage, not the compost. In the prairie settlers' early years, oranges were not available, so rhubarb gave similar health benefits. Women used the stalks in many ways in jam and in baking. Rhubarb freezes well, then cooks in a few minutes, with little or no water added. Watch so it doesn't burn. Add a little honey. Rhubarb can be mixed into apple sauce or crisp.

Strawberries: a warning – strawberries are among the top fruits most heavily sprayed with pesticides, and you cannot peel or scrub them. Non-organic apples are also heavily sprayed but can be peeled. Out-of-season strawberries probably come from South or Central America where pesticide use is even less controlled than in the United States and Canada. These poisons damage the plantation workers far more than the Canadian eaters. Of course we can console ourselves that **the super good all fruits do us, may somewhat counteract the pesticides, helping our bodies deal with the toxins**. Anyway, why must we have strawberries all year round? Let's wait for summer "real" berries to astonish us.

Fruits that are most heavily sprayed with up to 36 different types of pesticides are: strawberries, apples, peaches, imported grapes, cherries, nectarines, pears and raspberries. Also consider the damage to soil and water and air as well as to human workers. So try to buy organic local fruits, and plant a fruit tree, even on city spaces.

Bananas: Alas, it seems the fruit most destructive to the environment, and to the health of the workers, is our beloved banana, the world's number one favourite fruit. Like all southern plantations providing food for us, banana mono-crops have pushed local farmers off their lands so they can no longer grow a variety of food to feed their families. The chemical inputs (pesticides, etc.) poison the soil and the water, kill vital organisms, and severely sicken the workers. The massive chemical-laden banana wastes add extra poison to the waters. *Foro Emaus* is a grassroots ecumenical Costa Rican organization, struggling to improve conditions in the banana industry "for the defense of life."

So, caring for the Earth, if we must have a banana, let's try to eat organic. The growing conditions are better, especially if the bananas are fair trade. Better still, try to eat local fruit. And if you want potassium, note that 1 medium baked potato with skin gives nearly twice as much potassium as a large banana. Other local foods with more potassium than a banana include 1/2 cup (125 mL) cooked dry beans, 1 cup (250 mL) yogurt and 1 cup (250 mL) tomato juice.

Pesticides in Fruits and Vegetables

The Dirty Dozen Plus	The Clean Fifteen
Apples	Asparagus
Celery	Avocados
Cherry Tomatoes	Cabbage
Cucumbers	Canteloupe
Grapes	Cauliflower
Nectarines	Eggplant
Peaches	Grapefruit
Potatoes	Kiwi
Snap Peas	Mangoes
Spinach	Onions
Strawberries	Papayas
Sweet Bell Peppers	Pineapples
Hot Peppers	Sweet Corn
Kale / Collards	Sweet Peas
	Sweet Potatoes

Source: Environmental Working Group www.ewg.org

Grains, Seeds, Nuts

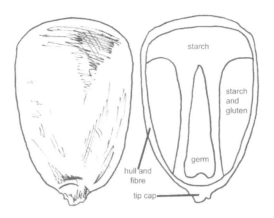

Whole grain includes the entire germ and bran of the grain. The bran is high in fibre, also has antioxidants and B vitamins. The germ (which grows into a new plant) is rich in healthy oils, B vitamins, minerals, and some protein. All these nutrients are linked with lowering obesity, lessening risk of heart disease, diabetes and cancer, and supplying more energy. By refining the grain to produce white flour or white rice, the bran and the germ are taken away. Sometimes a few vitamins are added back, "enriched", but this in no way makes up for what is lost. So white flour in most baked goods in the supermarket gives little nourishment.

Gluten-Free Grains (GF)

We can all benefit from the special gifts of these various grains, whether or not we have gluten sensitivity. Less gluten may be good for all of us. (Note that most modern wheat seed has been fortified with extra gluten.) Gluten-free grains include: quinoa, buckwheat (kasha), millet, rice (preferably brown rice), wild rice, amaranth, hemp and flax. All except rice are grown in the prairie provinces. As flour, these can be substituted for some of the wheat in baking. For gluten-free baking, include sweet rice flour - about 1/3 of the total flour - mixed with other gluten-free grains. This makes baking hold together well, compensating for the lack of gluten. Some pulses such

as chickpea, are also available as gluten-free flour which works well mixed with other flours, giving a little more texture.

When substituting for white flour in a recipe, reduce the heavier flours by 1 Tbsp (15 mL) per cup.

Amaranth has twice as much protein as rice, nine times more calcium than wheat, 40 times more calcium and four times more iron than rice, as promoted by Vandana Shiva in *Stolen Harvest.* Amaranth (not technically a grain) has more protein, calcium, magnesium, iron and fibre than other gluten-free "grains." Mixed with other gluten-free flours, amaranth gives a good texture to gluten-free baking.

Buckwheat has high protein and high fibre. In baking, blend it with lighter flour.

Kasha is buckwheat groats (kernels) toasted, giving a nutty flavour. Kasha is a basic food in Eastern Europe especially as kasha porridge (not Kashi packaged sugary cereal). Like quinoa and hemp, kasha is a nearly complete protein.

To cook kasha: rinse in a sieve, under the tap. Cover with double the amount of water. Simmer for 15 minutes, then let sit off heat, covered, for 10 minutes more. Save any excess water for stock. Use in place of rice. Any surplus can be saved in the fridge for 1 or 2 weeks, or for a long time in freezer. If we freeze the grains flat in zip plastic bags, it is easy to knock them loose as needed.

Millet, an ancient grain, is a staple in Asia and Africa, but is now grown in Saskatchewan and can be used in place of rice. Millet has more protein than brown rice, and cooks in less time. Millet is good for diabetics.

To cook millet: rinse with cool water through a fine sieve. Add 1/2 cup (125 mL) millet to 1 1/2 cup (375 mL) boiling water. Simmer for 20 minutes so it is fluffy and ready to eat.

Quinoa (KEEN-wah): cherished by the Inca, quinoa almost died out with the Spanish conquest but was recently re-discovered. Because quinoa was developed in the Andean mountains, it flourishes in drought-like conditions, and also has its own natural pesticide coating which is perfect for our prairies. Like most ancient grains, quinoa is highly nourishing, giving more nutritional value and energy than the same amounts of meat (without the health and ethical concerns of factory-farmed meat). Quinoa has a combination of most life-supporting nutrients, is easily digested, has "good" carbohydrates which digest slowly, and is ideal as a "first food" for babies, and for people with attention deficit disorder and autism.

Quinoa is kosher because it is not technically a grain; but to be kosher it must not grow near barley. Use as rice, in porridge and in salads. Quinoa flakes can replace rolled oats for gluten-free (GF) baking. We have learned that because quinoa has become so popular in the developed world, the price has soared. So some local poor people in Bolivia, Ecuador and Peru for whom quinoa has been a nourishing staple food, now cannot afford to eat it, and instead eat cheaper imported junk food. Some Andean land which once grew a variety of crops is being turned into quinoa monoculture. On the plus side, some Andean farmers can now get cash for their quinoa, which allows them to buy other nutritious food, transportation, medical care, and send their kids to school.

Saskatchewan-grown quinoa is available, but so far, the quinoa flour in one Regina Health Food store is grown in Ecuador and milled in B.C. Let's encourage our farmers to grow and mill our own local quinoa.

To cook quinoa: rinse in a fine sieve, then put 1 cup of quinoa into 2 cups (500 mL) of water. Bring to boil. Reduce heat to simmer and cook for 10 minutes. Then turn heat off, keep covered, still on the burner; let sit 4 to 7 minutes. Remove from burner and uncover. Makes 3 cups. You can store in fridge for a week, or freeze, ready when wanted.

Rice: growing rice has needed masses of water, but newer methods use less. Of course rice cannot be grown in Canada, so we prefer to eat local grains or Canadian potatoes, or mix rice with Saskatchewan wild rice. Rather than white rice, choose brown rice because of its nuttier flavour, texture and much greater nutrition. It is rich in minerals and vitamins, especially the B's and provides high-quality protein. *To cook rice*: use twice as much water as rice. Bring to boil, and then simmer about 30 minutes.

Teff is an African grain, grown mainly in Ethiopia. In Ethiopian restaurants, the flat bread, enjera, is made from teff. This ancient grass was domesticated as early as 4,000 BCE. Teff is gluten-free, high in protein, calcium, iron, fibre, and B vitamins. Teff flour is used in baking.

To cook teff: cook as you would cook quinoa. Add 1/2 cup (125 mL) to 2 cups (500 mL) water. Bring to boil, then simmer, 15-20 minutes or until water is absorbed. Use as you would use rice.

Wild Rice or Indian Rice, or Manomin (Anishnabe / Ojibway, Cree). Wild rice was and is a staple food honoured in legends, feasts and ceremonies by Aboriginal people in eastern parts of Canada and north-eastern parts of the U.S. It grows naturally in marshy areas. The seeds, a kind of grass, were introduced to Saskatchewan in the 1930's and now Saskatchewan is the largest producer in Canada, and the La Ronge Band is a leader in wild rice production. Wild rice has twice the protein of brown rice, no pesticides or gluten, and has a long shelf life (up to 10 years if kept dry).

To cook wild rice: wash 1 cup (250 mL) wild rice in a sieve under running water and stir into 4 cups (1 L) boiling water. Boil gently with lid on, 45 to 60 minutes until grains are open and soft. (Soak the rice overnight, and it will cook faster). It puffs up to 4 times the original size, and for fluffier rice, let it stand for 30 minutes before draining.

OR (less energy, more time) stir 1 cup (250 mL) wild rice into 4 cups (1 L) boiling water. Bring to brisk boil for 1 minute, turn down heat and simmer for 15 minutes. Turn off heat, keep lid on. Let sit for 1 1/2 hours or more. Drain and save any excess nutritious water for soup stock. Freeze surplus.

Let's aid our health, and support northern workers by eating more wild rice. Use in salad, stir fries, soup, or dessert, as you would use white rice, or mix with other rice or grains.

Grains with Gluten

Barley is an excellent source of insoluble fibre, also selenium and some minerals. Hulled barley is the most nutritious because it is "whole grain." Pearl barley has some layers removed.

To cook barley: rinse under running water. Add 1 part barley to 3 1/2 parts boiling water or broth. After it returns to boil, reduce heat, cover and simmer. Hulled barley takes 90 minutes; pearl barley takes 60 minutes. When cool, put into glass jars or flat plastic bags, ready for whenever you want it. Use as rice, toss into soups.

Wheat: the wheat widely used today, whether as flour for baking, or as packaged cookies, crackers, muffins, pasta or pizza, is not the life-building wheat our grandmothers knew. In the past 50 years, agro scientists have hybridized and crossbred wheat to greatly increase yields. That has caused a decrease in nutrition. Wheat is now bred to alter its natural gluten in order to increase its rising power. Modern wheat is the chief gluten-sensitivity culprit. Modern wheat is unique among modern grains in its ability to convert quickly to blood sugar. This in turn increases diabetes risk and weight gain. Some doctors report that patients who severely cut out wheat, lose unwanted fat and greatly improve their general health, as told by William Davis in his 2012 book *Wheat Belly*.

The heritage Red Fife wheat is being revived on the prairies and makes delicious bread, even with no white flour added – because it is usually high in gluten. But still it seems to be well tolerated by people with sensitivities. Canadian heritage Red Fife wheat is certified organic. **Canadian wheat has not been genetically modified but American wheat has.**

Spelt and **kamut** have a little gluten as they are part of the wheat family. However, they have not been hybridized as modern wheat has. Hybridization, in order to increase crop yields and lower the height of growth also results in decreased nutrition. Spelt and kamut are more easily digested than modern wheat, and are highly nutritious. Kamut is labelled Polish Wheat in some Health Food stores. Both make good substitutes for modern wheat in baking.

Seeds and Nuts

Chia seeds are native to Mexico and Guatemala and were as important as corn to the Aztecs. Today chia is grown commercially in Mexico, Guatemala, Nicaragua, Bolivia, Argentina, and especially in Australia. Chia is high in calcium, protein, Omega-3 fatty acids, manganese and phosphorous. Chia seeds improve blood pressure, stabilize blood sugar and strengthen bones and teeth. Try chia seeds and give thanks for this gift from Indigenous Central Americans.

Flax seed is high in fibre, also loaded with nutrients, especially Omega-3 fatty acids and lignans (antioxidants). Research is showing that flax may help protect against heart disease, cancer, stroke and diabetes. Flax seeds need to be crushed to let the nutrients out, unless you want them only as roughage for your body's plumbing! You can buy ground flax seed, but it is preferable to buy whole seeds and grind them in a coffee grinder or blender. Ground flax has a short shelf life, so grind only a small amount at a time. Flax grows happily in south-central Saskatchewan, gladdening our eyes with fields of blue.

Hemp is a top super health food. Hulled hemp seeds ("hemp hearts") are high in protein and easily digested. Hemp also contains all of the essential amino acids and essential fatty acids necessary to sustain healthy human life. Hulled hemp is especially high in vitamin E and many minerals. Hemp is gluten-free, GMO-free, pesticide-free and also THC-free, so is NOT MARIJUANA! Hemp seeds are delicious. Sprinkle on cereal, salad, pasta and dessert; add to baking and smoothies. Hemp seeds give the most benefits if they are uncooked. Store in the fridge.

"Hemp is great for losing weight because it fills you up. Take 1 or 2 Tbsp (15-30 mL) a day. Hemp can provide a nearly perfect diet along with fruit, vegetables and yogurt. It's a cheap and easy high nutrition food source for all people, especially the poor" says Travis Treso of Hemp Haven, Regina.

Pumpkin seeds are an immune booster and an antioxidant. They are a good source of zinc and vitamin E, protein, bone-building magnesium, phosphorus, manganese and iron. They can be stored in the fridge up to 2 months in an airtight container. Roasting for 15 minutes at 170°F (75°C) brings out the full flavour of the seed.

Sunflower seeds are very high in the antioxidant vitamin E, plus a wide combination of other vitamins and minerals; including substances that reduce stress, increase brain function and help protect against heart disease and cancer. Look for raw seeds with no oil or salt added. Toast briefly in a toaster oven if you wish. Toss into salads, yogurt, muffins or porridge.

Sesame seeds contain more protein than any nut, and have as much iron as liver. They are high in vitamin E and calcium. Tahini is sesame butter and can be made at home in a food processor. For my morning shot of calcium, I spread tahini on whole grain bread with a little local fruit "spread."

Almonds: most almonds come from California. They are high in monounsaturated fats, which are linked to lower risk of heart disease. When eaten with skins on, they provide a high dose of vitamin E. Almonds are rich in calcium, high in magnesium which improves the flow of blood and nutrients through the body, and high in potassium which is essential for normal blood pressure. After a high sugar meal, gobble some almonds to keep blood sugar down. Select whole, unsalted, raw organic almonds. Enjoy roasted as snacks or spread almond butter on toast.

The bad news is that bees rented from bee farmers are transported from all over the United States to pollinate California's almond trees. Non-organic trees are heavily sprayed with toxins, which have probably contributed to the massive death and disappearance of many bees. Try to eat organic almonds. Read more about **Bees in Chapter 4.**

Herbs and Spices

Honour the hidden powers of herbs and spices. Breathe in the special aroma of each one.

Crush dry herbs by rubbing them in your palms before adding to a mixture to release the flavour. 1 Tbsp (15 mL) fresh herb equals 1 tsp (5 mL) dry herb.

Caraway has been used since the Stone Age in Europe, Asia and North Africa. Caraway is suited to the prairie climate, surviving through the winter to produce seeds in its second year. Caraway is high in protein and fat. It has been valued for easing a host of ailments, including bronchitis, coughs, and digestive complaints. Caraway adds a unique flavour to bannock, rye bread, sauerkraut and soups.

Chives give a wealth of benefits. Chop small, and add at the last minute to soups, egg dishes, salads, dips, potatoes or as a classy garnish. The flowers, sprinkled on salad, give a special zing.

Cinnamon is thought to have secret powers, especially when part-nered with honey. Cinnamon is the bark of wild trees native to the Caribbean, South America, China and Ceylon (source of the common cinnamon). Cinnamon has been used as medicine in Egypt as early as 2,000 BCE. Today it is used to help many ailments including infections and the common cold. Studies show that cinnamon regulates blood sugar, reduces bad cholesterol, preserves food, helps relieve arthritis pain and menstrual pain, holds promise for helping people with Alzheimer's disease and Multiple Sclerosis. Sprinkle freely on plain yogurt, porridge, fruit dessert and other foods.

Basil is a powerful antioxidant, eases inflammation (as aspirin does), and aids short-term memory. To eat, pile on lots, especially with tomatoes, sandwiches, salads, soups, stews, in salad dressings, and pesto. Basil should not be stored in the fridge because the cold turns the leaves black. Easily dried and enjoyed all winter.

Cilantro / Coriander: this double-personality plant is easily grown. Cilantro is the leaf, which gives a distinctive flavour to Asian and other soups. In Mexico, tomatoes are eaten with cilantro leaves. Coriander is the seed of the plant, refreshing to chew after a meal; seeds can be ground in a blender to make a coarse powder used in spicy soups and stews along with cumin.

Dill pops up all through the garden, once a few seeds are scattered. This useful herb can enhance most foods. Add whole to boiling potatoes or turnip, then mash, or roast whole in the oven or on a grill, to become mellower and oh so delicious.

Ginger root adds zip and health wherever it goes. Ginger reduces motion sickness and nausea, improves digestion and strengthens the heart. It may help to prevent serious illnesses. Scrub the ginger root, cut into chunks, and store in a glass jar or bag in the freezer (to prevent drying up). For use, scrape skin off and grate or chop fine. Add to soup, muffins, fish and whatever seems worth a try. For stir-fries and egg dishes, add ginger root with onions to the sauté at the beginning. To ease a cold, simmer pieces of ginger root 20 minutes (no need to peel). Add a taste of honey and sip!

Mint comes in several varieties such as peppermint and chocolate and is easy to grow. Mint has long been grown and valued around the world. Mint dries well for winter use, but the fresh leaves are most beneficial. Mint makes lovely tea, soothes stomachs and flagging spirits, aids digestion, nausea, asthma, fatigue, gastrointestinal disorders, and memory problems. Add to salads, lamb, vegetables such as carrots, and desserts.

Miso is a health food originating from Japan. The salty brownish paste is made from soybeans or barley or other grains, and sea salt, and is fermented. The fermentation produces an enzyme-rich food, known to promote health. Miso detoxifies the body from pollutant chemicals. Use miso in soups, salad dressings and vegetable dishes. It can replace bouillon. Barley miso is made in B.C.

Mustard: most commercial mustard in the world is grown in Saskatchewan, then shipped away for processing, then sent back to us. But now, specialty mustard processed in Saskatchewan is becoming available. It is curcumin that makes turmeric and mustard so boldly yellow, and is an antioxidant and anti-inflammatory agent.

Oregano is Nature's antibiotic, protecting against bacteria, viruses, fungi and parasites. Oregano is easy to grow and survives prairie winters. To dry, hang up a tied bunch in a cool, dark place, not in direct sun. Store in glass jars. Use in soups, stews, and salads.

Parsley is a diuretic that won't deplete the body of potassium and other nutrients, has powerful anti-cancer properties, and cleanses the blood. So eat up that colourful touch on your plate – it is not just decoration but tastes good too! Parsley is easily grown in a balcony pot.

Rosemary has feathery leaves. This ancient herb carries legends and healing uses. It perks up foods like potatoes, squash and meat. We can keep rosemary in a pot indoors in winter, then transfer that pot outdoors for summer. Keep the plant moist at all times. Dried rosemary leaves store well and keep their flavour.

Sage is a sturdy plant which survives through prairie winters. In the fall, snip off most of the little branches and hang inside to dry. Store in a glass bottle ready for winter use in roasting chicken, stuffing, soups and herbed scones. Indigenous peoples on the prairie consider wild sage to be sacred. So we give thanks when picking – as we should with all plants.

Tarragon has a strong flavour, so if you like it, you use it a lot. French tarragon is best. Try with chicken, egg dishes, sauces and marinades, with yogurt and cucumber raita. If you're lucky, tarragon will survive outdoors all winter. It does not do well in wet soil or indoors.

Thyme is an antiseptic. It is also effective in easing gastro-intestinal complaints, peps up scrambled egg and soup and grows easily. Dry for winter use.

Turmeric is thought to be a reason cancer was rarer in India, because of its active ingredient curcumin. But with the coming of a more Western diet, cancer is also rising in India. Turmeric is a strong anti-inflammatory, an anti-bacterial and a liver detoxifier. It is also considered useful against arthritis pain and depression. Turmeric gives most benefit if first mixed with a bit of oil before adding to other food. Turmeric has little taste, but a strong yellow colour. It can go into soup, stews, smoothies, and egg dishes. I put a small spoonful into my porridge or scrambled egg each day. Friends swear by their daily turmeric dose to ease their pain.

Herbs grow well in pots on a balcony. Some, like parsley, thyme, rosemary and chives brought indoors, will continue growing by an indoor sunny window through the winter. Tiny onion or garlic bulbs, planted in a pot indoors in fall, grow tasty spears to liven up winter soup.

Pulses

Pulses include lentils, chickpeas, beans, dry peas – but not soy! 67% of the world's lentils are grown in Saskatchewan and they are Saskatchewan's health superstars. Canada is the world's largest exporter of pulses which are exported to be staple food in the Middle East, Pakistan and India as well as to South America and Europe.

Pulses are high in protein (20 to 25%) so are listed as a meat alternative in the Canada Food Guide. Pulses are gluten-free, low in fat and calories (unlike peanuts and soybeans). Pulses are high in fibre, so they protect against many ills. Pulses are high in complex carbohydrates (the good kind the body absorbs slowly). Canadian pulses are not genetically modified. Pulses are part of the legume family, which enrich the soil with nitrogen, helping fertilize the soil naturally.

Lentils boost iron. Lentils are high in potassium, which counteracts the damaging effect of salt, and so can lower blood pressure. Of all plant foods, lentils contain the most folate, a B-vitamin especially important for pregnant women, also for preventing heart attack or stroke. The tiny orange-coloured "crimson split lentils" are really the dark "red lentils," with the hull removed.

On New Year's Day, Italian Canadians eat lentils for good luck. Smart Idea!

Eat up! How?

Rinse under running water and pick over. Soak most pulses in lots of water overnight, then throw away the soaking water.

If gas is a problem, change soaking water during a long soak, and do not use soaking water for cooking. You can add a chunk of whole ginger to the soaking and cooking water, and then remove. Cook thoroughly.

When cooked, freeze some 1 or 2 cup (250 - 500 mL) quantities in a jar, leaving 1/2 inch clear at the top, OR in sealed plastic bags (pile flat to save freezer space).

Pulses can then be added to soup, salad, stir-fry, stew, spaghetti sauce and omelets. Pulses can be mashed or puréed smooth for dips, wraps, or baking.

Cooking methods & times for dry pulses							
	Beans	Whole peas	Split peas	Whole Lentils	Split Lentils	Whole Chickpeas	Split Chickpeas
Rinse	Yes	Yes	Yes	Yes	Yes	Yes	Yes
Soak	Yes	Yes	No	No	No	Yes	No
Amount of water per 1 cup (250 mL) dry pulses	2 ½ - 3 cups (625 to 750 mL)	2 ½ - 3 cups (625 to 750 mL)	2 cups (500 mL)	2 ½ - 3 cups (625 to 750 mL)	2 cups (500 mL)	2 ½ - 3 cups (625 to 750 mL)	2 cups (500 mL)
Cooking Time	1 – 1½ hrs	1½ – 2 hrs	45 min	10 – 30 min	5 – 15 min	1½ – 2 hrs	½ – 1 hr
Pressure cook time (at 15 psi)*	8 – 12 min	5 -7 min	No	No	No	12 – 15 min	5 – 7 min
Yield from 1 cup (250 mL) dry pulses	2½ cups (625 mL)	2½ cups (625 mL)	2 cups (500 mL)	2½ cups (625 mL)	2 cups (500 mL)	2½ cups (625 mL)	2 cups (500 mL)

*Pressure cook times are for pulses that have been pre-soaked and are based on the "quick" or "cold water" release method, in which the pressure cooker is placed in cold water after removing from the burner to lower pressure. If a "natural" release method is used instead (pressure is left to fall on its own), the cooking times need to be reduced.

Pulses: Cooking with beans, peas, lentils and chickpeas, p. 10. Reprinted with permission from Pulse Canada. www.pulsecanada.com

Pulse Purée: place home-cooked or canned (rinsed and drained) pulses into a blender. For every cup (250 mL) cooked pulses, add 1/4 cup (60 mL) water. Blend to make a smooth purée, adding 1 Tbsp (15 mL) water at a time if needed. Purées can be frozen and kept for several months in the freezer. OR when baking, just throw the cooked lentils into the blender with the other ingredients being blended.

For **slow cooker** recipes, beans already soaked should be boiled 10-12 minutes in fresh water before adding to the crock pot.

Sprouting: all whole pulses, being seeds, can be sprouted. Lentils are the easiest seed to sprout, for a bonus burst of health. **See Chapter 9: Sprouts.**

Pulse Flours are in some Health Food stores and are especially useful for gluten-free baking.

These two organizations have excellent information:

Saskatchewan Pulse Growers
www.saskpulse.com, lentil@saskpulse.com

Pulse Canada (in Winnipeg)
www.pulsecanada.com, office@pulsecanada.com

Soy Beans are not pulses. Soy beans and the products processed from soy beans – tofu, soy milk – are not included in our recipes. All soy beans (unless organic) are genetically modified, thus believed to have negative health and environmental impacts. Contrary to the powerful soy industry's propaganda, only fermented soy creates health-promoting probiotics (as in miso, tempeh and soy sauce). Most of our soy products (tofu, oil, soy milk, cheese, burgers, ice-cream and snacks) are processed from non-fermented soy. In her controversial book *The Whole Soy Story: the Dark Side of America's Favorite Health Food*, Kayla Daniel reports on thousands of studies which link unfermented soy to breast cancer and brain damage, as well as to digestive distress, immune system breakdown, thyroid dysfunction, reproductive disorders, infant abnormalities and severe food allergies. UTNE Reader says that Asians traditionally ate about 9 grams of soy products a day, mostly fermented, with only a little tofu. In North America, one soy snack can contain 20 grams of non-fermented soy protein.

Even more important, non-organic soy beans are grown in massive GMO monocultures, depleting the soil even in Saskatchewan. Much of the world's soy bean crops are grown where once stood rainforests – our oxygen source and carbon sink, as well as home to myriad plants and creatures who held unknown blessings for humans, now lost to soy bean monoculture.

Let's stick to local pulses which give well-being.

Sprouts

"A seed is the living germ of the plant; all of its nutrients and energy are stored in it. When we sprout it, it comes alive; its vitality is released and its nutrients multiply. This life force is given to our body cells... to promote wellness," writes Lucie Desjarlais, in her booklet *The Wonders of Sprouting.*

Forget far-imported, non-nutritional winter lettuce. Sprouts are super easy, low cost, and fun. Sprouts are powerhouses of concentrated nutrition, created by the living process of germination. Proteins, vitamins, enzymes, minerals and trace elements are many times more concentrated in the sprout than in the mature plant. If you grow this super-food yourself you know it is fresh, it does far less damage to the Earth than commercially grown and imported food, and is also very low-cost.

Tools
Glass jar (16 oz pint size or 32 oz quart size)
Tin lid (holes punched with a nail)
Tiny seeds need a square of nylon stocking or net, secured with an elastic band.
Purchased seed-sprouting equipment is also popular.

Seeds

Larger seeds like lentils and garbanzo (chick peas) can be ordinary organic ones from a Health Food store, but small seeds should be intended for sprouting. The easiest sprouts to grow (ready in 3 days) are: lentil, red clover, mung beans (keep mung in the dark so they do not become bitter). Sunflower seeds produce larger leaves, fine greens for salads.

Process

1 or 2 Tbsp seeds (15 or 30 mL) - rinse well and put into a jar.

Cover with water and fasten lid or net securely.

Soak for 6 to 12 hours (depending on size of seed; broccoli seed needs no more than 2 hours).

Pour off soaking water (save for another use).

Rinse once or twice a day by pouring on fresh water, swirl, then pouring off. Shake well.

Set jar upside down on an angle in a bowl small enough to keep the jar tilted to drain off all water.

Store on the counter.

When white tails appear, put near a window (never in direct sun) to develop the leaves.

It's time to start munching.

When sprouts are grown enough, store them in the fridge for up to 2 weeks. Rinse every 2 days.

How to use: just munch or add to smoothies, scrambled eggs, sandwiches, burritos, stir fries, soup, stews and salads. For cookies or muffins chop the sprouts, and then blend in with the egg mixture. Crunchy lentil sprouts can take the place of walnuts.

Tips

I use the water drained off my sprouts each day for soup stock, porridge or house plants.

If we sometimes miss a rinsing, it's O.K.

Plants will die if roots are left standing in water, or if they are too hot.

It is better to grow seeds in glass rather than plastic, as plastic is known to leach dangerous elements.

You can also sprout tiny seeds in 1 inch of soil or growing mix in a small plastic tub with drainage holes punched in the bottom. Set container on a jar ring to allow more air circulation (these will grow up straight, not "little wigglies" as my children called the jar-sprouted ones).

Watch how to do it on the web at www.sprouting.com.

Read how to do it: *The Wonders of Sprouting* by Lucie Desjarlais, nutritionist. Available through Mumm's.

Buy fresh sprouts at the Farmers' Market.

Order seeds from Mumm's Sprouting Seeds, www.sprouting.com.

Be part of Nature's magic happening.

Sweets and Salt

Sweets

Cane sugar for us is grown on land which could otherwise be growing food for people in the developing world. Many sugar cane labourers work and live under abominable conditions. Sugar cane and corn need more fertilizers, pesticides and irrigation than any other field crops. Processing sugar cane into our sugar requires various chemicals. Brown sugar is no more "natural" than white, because it goes through the same process with the addition of natural molasses, which had been removed. Learn more by watching the film *The Price of Sugar.*

Carob is often used as a chocolate substitute; lower in calories, naturally sweeter, without the caffeine and additives found in cheap chocolate. Carob has been prized for 3,000 years in the Mediterranean, and now can grow in the southern U.S. Carob is high in calcium, vitamins B and A, can halt serious diarrhea and helps relieve nausea. We can substitute carob powder for an equal amount of cocoa (but reduce the sugar in the recipe), or use carob chips instead of chocolate.

Chocolate: most cocoa beans are grown in West Africa; some are still grown in Central America and in Mexico where the Mayans developed them. The good news is chocolate and cocoa are good for us – if from organic, raw dark chocolate. Organic dark chocolate has much less sugar (the bitterer, the better!), no milk or other toxic additives. Less-processed, organic, dark chocolate cocoa has been shown to lower blood pressure, reduce risk of colon cancer, provide healthy fats, be an anti-depressant, improve brain function, and enhance glucose metabolism (which helps diabetes). Cocoa is considered to have 1% caffeine, compared to 4% in tea and over 10% in coffee.

Ancient South and Central American Indigenous farmers transformed the cacao bean into cocoa, the highly prized luxury drink of the Mayan and Aztec nobility. The Mayans honoured their cacao god with sacred ritual. In the Philippines where cacao spread very early, the hill people honour their mountain goddess Maria Cacao.

Today, if our cocoa and chocolate are Fair Trade, they give farmers a fair wage, allow children to go to school instead of labouring in cocoa plantations, perhaps even as slaves. Without fair trade, growers have no bargaining power and earn about one penny for the chocolate in one average chocolate bar. Fair Trade also encourages sustainable growing methods.

Corn Syrup: AVOID. High fructose corn syrup is thought to be a major cause of the obesity plague. Unlike sucrose, which triggers appetite stop-signs in the body, fructose tells eaters to keep on going. Especially for children, their high-fructose intake affects their mood and attention span as well as their weight. Because in the U.S. corn is heavily subsidized, fructose from corn is cheap (also addictive), so it is sneaked into most items on supermarket shelves, and massively poured into soft drinks. Read the fine print!

Honey (local): contains antioxidants, helps digestion, provides essential nutrients, and helps the body absorb calcium. Honey is also a natural antiseptic, keeping wounds and burns free of infection. It takes far less energy to produce honey than to refine and transport sugar from sugarcane. Honey needs no refining step. Canadian beekeepers leave almost no environmental footprint. And beekeepers, especially on organic farms, are taking care of the bees. Buying local honey supports local beekeepers and strengthens our food security.

Bees are providing one-third of our food, by pollinating the plants, and in their life-process, creating both honey and wax. Let's light our meals with beeswax candles, thus supporting the bee farmers and purifying the air (not polluting like the usual petroleum kind).

Maple Syrup: when I want sweetener I add 100% authentic maple syrup or local honey. Pure maple syrup contains many compounds beneficial to health; it is high in antioxidants and anti-inflammatory properties, plus important natural minerals, but it is a sugar so go easy! Most of our Canadian maple syrup comes from Quebec or Ontario, but also Saskatchewan maple syrup is being made from Manitoba maple trees. AVOID imitation maple syrup made of high-fructose corn syrup.

Sugar: annual sugar consumption per North American has risen from 17.5 lbs in 1915 to 150 lbs in 2011. Diagnosed diabetes has spiked from 2% of the population (U.S.) in 1973, to 7% in 2010. *"Excessive sugar isn't just empty calories, it's toxic... Manufacturers use sugar to replace taste in foods bled of fat so that they seem more healthful,* *such as fat-free baked goods, which often contain large quantities of added sugar,"* reports the *National Geographic,* August 2013. Sugar is not only addictive, but saps energy, making exercise more difficult.

Sugar Substitutes: AVOID. Many have been implicated in possibly causing cancer and other serious diseases, such as Alzheimer's and blindness. The unhealthiest are considered to be Saccharin, Aspartame and Sucralose. Healthier sugar substitutes start with eating fewer sweets; our taste buds can adjust! Substitute whole fruit, low-sweet organic fruit toppings and dried fruits; also sweet vegetables such as carrot, parsnip, sweet potatoes and beets. **Stevia**, a completely safe herb from the South American stevia plant, is a totally natural, low-calorie sweetener and a little goes a long way. Fruit sugars are in all fresh fruits and pure fruit juices. Raisins, dates, dried apricots and prunes are unsweetened whole foods. Try to use organic as both the sugars in dried fruits and the pesticides on the fruits are concentrated.

Things are getting tough for me
Can't eat beef – mad cow disease
Can't eat chicken – bird flu
Can't eat eggs – salmonella
Can't eat fish – heavy metals in water
Can't eat vegetables – pesticides sprayed on everything
So I do believe that leaves chocolate
Hurray for CHOCOLATE!
– Old Man

Salt (sodium)

We need some salt, but pre-packaged processed foods contain overdoses of salt, enticing people to buy more, because salt is addictive. Salt can also be used to mask ingredients that get into the food during processing. All this extra salt is linked to high blood pressure, heart attacks and strokes. Learn more from Michael Moss in his 2013 book *Salt, Sugar, Fat: How the Food Giants Tricked Us.*

To reduce salt intake: **cut down or avoid** processed smoked meats (they also have damaging nitrates), junk snack food, salad dressings, pickles, canned and dried food such as soups, monosodium glutamate (MSG is used in much but not all Chinese food), soy sauce and restaurant soup – all very high in salt. **Enjoy** a host of other flavours, with herbs and spices; make your own herb mixes with just a little sea salt. **Read** the labels. **Rinse** canned vegetables. **Halve** the salt in most recipes – it will be fine. There is no need to add salt to cooking water. **Urge** our governments to compel reduction of salt in processed foods, as other governments have done. **Complain** to restaurants about the unnecessary salt in foods, or avoid the restaurants, but tell them why.

Sea salt is gathered by evaporation of seawater, often still by a family business, so it has the original minerals. Sea salt is credited with many health benefits, but no definitive testing has been done and pollution in the sea may become a problem. Regular rock salt is mined from underground, and then processed, removing important trace minerals, adding additives including iodine and aluminum.

Vegetables

Glory in the riot of colour – and health.

> *"Lack of enough vegetables is a major cause of deaths by cancer, heart disease and stroke"* – the United Nations

> *"Vegetables are crucial for child mental and physical development and for disease prevention. Eating sustainably-grown vegetables protects the environment, preserves biodiversity, brings food security despite changing climate. Vegetables can withstand drought better than staple crops like wheat, because with shorter growing time, vegetables can make best use of scarce water supplies and soil*

nutrients. Growing vegetables can be an affordable way to increase nutrition and income." – Danielle Nierenberg, Food Tank

It is best to buy lots in season, local and preferably organic; then freeze or preserve in jars. Or buy frozen: because they are quick-frozen, they are often fresher than "fresh" produce which has travelled a great distance and been in storage.

Aliums: Onions, chives, leeks, garlic are super health-givers and garden protectors.

Arugula is one of the dark green leafy vegetables with a spicy taste; also known as Rocket. Like all leafy greens, arugula is high-fibre and nutrient-rich. Arugula is loaded with vitamins B, C, A and K (which helps the body absorb calcium). Arugula is a brassica/cruciferous vegetable (like cabbage, broccoli, and kale) and so is high in cancer preventing phytochemicals. Mix with lettuces, the darker the better. Add to salads and sandwiches.

Asparagus is a good source of fibre, folic acid, vitamins C, E, B6. It is used for treatment of many health problems such as urinary tract infections, nerve pain, AIDS and cancer. Most imported asparagus is grown in Peru. This vast monoculture crop is grown in a desert and depends totally on irrigation. Our imported out-of-season luxury food is draining Peru's wells dry, leading to a severe water crisis, especially for the small farmers. Let's wait for our springtime treat of our own fresh guilt-free asparagus.

Beets are high in many vitamins and minerals, especially vitamin B and iron, which is important for pregnant women. Beets cleanse the liver, purify the blood, help depression and lower blood pressure, plus are a high source of energy with "good" sugar, which is absorbed slowly.

To cook beets: scrub well with a brush and cut off the rough top. Roast beets in the oven for about 45 minutes, or boil until soft, saving the cooking water for baking, borscht, or a red smoothie. There is no need to remove the skin if beets are organic; but if you want to, dump hot beets into cold water, then grasp each beet, sliding the skin off. Cooked beets can be pickled or frozen whole. Raw beets can be eaten as beet sticks, or grated into salads.

Cherish the beet greens, an excellent source of carotenoids, antioxidants and vitamin A.

Storing: Separate leaves and stems from the roots, wash, wrap in cloth, and then put into a plastic bag in fridge. While still fresh, steam leaves and stems too for a few minutes in a little water. Beetroot can keep in the fridge for a few weeks.

Cabbage Family (cruciferous or brassica) are nutritional queens, high in vitamin C, beta-carotene and other protective compounds. These cabbage family super-vegetables help to fight off cancer and heart disease, fortify the immune system, and do many other good deeds, even neutralizing some toxins in cigarette smoke and city pollution. We are advised to eat cabbage after an x-ray. It is best to eat raw or gently steamed to preserve the vitamin C.

Bok Choy is a small Asian green, easy to grow and exceptional when stir-fried.

Broccoli: this super food is also high in calcium. Steam in a tiny bit of water or on top of other vegetables for only 2 or 3 minutes, and then take off the heat.

Brussels Sprouts ("baby cabbages") have even 4 times more vitamin C than their cabbage cousins. Marvel at their design on the stalk.

Kale is a best buy of imported (organic) winter greens. Its dark colour is a clue that kale is loaded with good stuff. It keeps well in the fridge. Add to salads or stir-fries, or steam with garlic, onion and a drop of tamari. Save the tough spine for soup stock. Kale keeps eyes keen – like any vegetable with beta-carotene. Also kale has the other virtues of the Cabbage family.

Frozen Kale

Get kale fresh from the farm for the most nutrients and save that super summer farm kale to enjoy its health boost in the winter.

Remove the tough part of spine and save it in the freezer for making stock. Wash kale leaves and chop. Steam/cook in boiling water for 2 minutes.

Drain and transfer to ice water for 2 minutes, spin in a salad spinner and lay on a towel and gently squeeze out the remaining water.

Spread kale over a sheet of parchment or waxed paper on a cookie sheet.

Leave in the freezer for at least 30 minutes.

Separate the kale, put in freezer bags, ready for adding to dishes as needed.

Carrots: let's cut up and eat our own local farmers' carrots, and also freeze them for the winter. They give loads of carotene, an antioxidant that can be changed by the body into vitamin A, which is especially good for our eyes and heart. The body can more easily absorb carrots' nutrients if cooked.

Celery: studies show that eating 2 stalks a day can lower blood pressure significantly, and is advised by naturopaths. The leaves have even more calcium, iron, potassium and vitamins A and C than the stalk BUT celery is one of the most highly pesticide-laden of all vegetables, so try to get organic, especially from local Farmers' Markets. Chop the leaves into salads and soup. Dry the leaves for winter and use as a substitute for celery stalk in cooking. Celery is a good finger-snack stuffed with goat cheese or hummus.

Chives are the first exciting greens of spring, and so easy to grow. Beg a little clump to plant in a corner of your yard and it happily spreads; or scatter a seed head for next year. In the garden chives deter unwanted pests, and chives will keep on giving, even in an indoor sunny window. Like other members of the allium family – garlic, onion, leek, scallion – chives give a wealth of benefits such as vitamins; especially vitamins C and A. Chives can also lower blood pressure and cholesterol, help in absorbing food nutrients and get rid of harmful bacteria in the intestinal tract. Cut chives 1 inch from the ground, chop small, and add at the last minute to soups, egg dishes, salads, dips, potatoes or as a classy garnish. The charming flowers are edible for humans and a delight for bees. To freeze: wash, pat dry, chop in 1/3 inch pieces, spread on a cookie tray in the freezer until frozen, then package.

Corn: when Columbus arrived on the shores of America he found cornfields 18 miles long. Even today, corn grown from traditional seeds is revered as a supreme food gift of the Corn Goddess, or the Creator (Iroquois and Chippewa). But corn has become a prime target of the chemical corporations' drive to increase profits. Nearly all commercial corn has been treated with the corporations' chemicals, so it can withstand ever more pesticides. Hybrid seeds cannot reproduce so farmers are compelled to keep buying the corporations' GM seeds, at rising prices. Corn in some form is in most of the packaged items on supermarket shelves, often as high fructose (very fattening) sugar or corn syrup. Get out your magnifying glass to check the fine print! When commercial corn has had the germ removed, it can last longer, but has lost most of its nutrition. What an insult to the great Corn Goddess! If we want corn we should get it from a Health Food store or a local organic farmer (cut off the niblets and freeze).

Corn (maize) gifted from the ancient Indigenous Americans has become the staple in Africa. That continent is suffering from Western agribusiness pressures including seeds, fertilizers and pesticides that are not suited to the land or the people, and now suffering severe drought. But the people's traditional conservation farming practices and their traditional crops are being revived, aided by some NGO's (Non-Government Organizations) with great success. An example is the Canadian Foodgrains Bank short film about conservation farming: *Maize and Mulch in Zimbabwe*. To find this film, search the title on the internet.

40% of U.S. corn is now grown for biofuels, to feed cars rather than people or animals. This creates severe food shortages, soaring food prices and great unrest throughout the world.

Cucumber: eat the peel for its fibre to reduce constipation and remove toxins that might lead to colon cancer. Cucumber has vital minerals and is also rich in potassium and magnesium to help lower blood pressure. Cucumber is high in vitamin K, is linked to bone strength; also is used to limit damage in the brains of Alzheimer's patients.

Garlic has been used as a cure-all since ancient times. Leading ethno-botanist Dr. James Duke, an expert on medicinal plants, places garlic among the world's best all-around plant medicines. Garlic has compounds helpful for more than 200 ailments. Garlic is the best plant for stimulating the immune system, relieves high blood pressure, and helps prevent heart disease and cancer. Garlic's goodness is released when the clove is cut and crushed. To prepare, chop off a tiny bit of the clove's end (not the tip). Chop small and crush. Add to just about everything. Add whole to boiling potatoes or turnip, then mash, or roast whole in the oven or on a grill, to become mellower and oh so delicious.

Leeks belong often in our diet. Before cooking, let them sit for at least 5 minutes after cutting, to improve their health gifts. Leeks have vitamin K, A, C and B6, and give iron, magnesium and fibre. Leeks support the health of blood vessels and cells; protect against cancers, decrease inflammation, help diabetes and strengthen the voice.

To cook leeks: cut up the inner leaves and sauté in broth on medium heat for 4 minutes; reduce heat and sauté another 3 minutes. Toss with 2 Tbsp (30 mL) Extra Virgin Olive Oil, 1 tsp (5 mL) lemon juice, sea salt or Himalayan salt and seasonings to taste. Combine with other foods. Leeks are especially good with thyme, fennel or mustard. After cooking, leeks will keep in the fridge only 1-2 days; frozen, up to 3 months. To store before cooking, keep unwashed and untrimmed in fridge up to 1-2 weeks.

Mushrooms are fungi and the ones in the grocery stores are often organic. Mushrooms are another traditional healing food, believed to help in combating cancer, heart disease, viral infections and autoimmune diseases. Mushrooms are one of the few foods that contain vitamin D, help the body absorb calcium, and boost our immune system. To use, do not soak in water because they soak up water like a sponge, but wipe with a damp cloth. Add to salads, stir fries, and many recipes, or munch raw. Portobello mushrooms are a good substitute for meat, in burgers and sandwiches. Saskatchewan boasts wild morels, but be careful, as some wild mushrooms are deadly.

Bell Peppers come in many colours including red, green, yellow and purple. Green peppers are just unripe red peppers, and compared to green peppers, red peppers have twice as much vitamin C and 10 times as much vitamin A, so are packed with antioxidants. Red peppers give more vitamin C than citrus fruits of equal weight and are also high in vitamin B6 and magnesium so help with anxiety and hypertension. All bell peppers contain lecithin which helps protect the eyes from cataracts and macular degeneration. The white membrane in peppers (also in citrus fruits) is high in vitamin P (a bioflavonoid). Peppers can be chopped and frozen "as is" (don't blanch).

Potatoes: the Inca and other Indigenous farmers of the Andes developed about 3,000 different varieties of potatoes, each suited to the particular needs of a specific locale. Even today, a field of potatoes produces more food and more nutrition more reliably and with less labour than wheat, with none of the extensive milling and processing. Thus potatoes cause less climate-changing emissions than would the same field planted in any grain. Potatoes are high in vitamin C and fibre, and a medium baked potato with skin on has nearly twice the potassium as one large banana. The problem with this staple food is the way we eat it, as fries, chips or hash browns. But eat them guilt-free: baked, roasted, steamed or boiled in only a little water. If organic, keep the skins on for the antioxidants, flavonoids and fibre in skin. If they are not organic, it is best to peel them because they are heavily sprayed and the chemicals collect just under the skin.

Radish roots are high in vitamin C, protein and calcium, while radish leaves are even higher. Radish is a detoxifier, cancer fighter, kidney cleaner, and helps in weight loss. Raw radish adds zip to salads, but if it is too hot for you, chop into soup or stew, or roast for a tiny bit of bite.

Spinach is loaded with health-giving nutrients. One cup gives as much calcium as a serving of yogurt. Use in salads instead of almost useless iceberg lettuce, or steam briefly. Mixed with dandelion leaves it is even more nutritious. Plant spinach in the fall to come up early in spring (even in cold Regina).

Squash: summer squash like **zucchini** and patty pan (the small frilly yellow one) contain a lot of water (which we need in summer), are high in magnesium which helps to reduce blood pressure. Zucchini are anti-inflammatory and anti-oxidant, low in calories and high in fibre. Serve as sticks in salad, or slice into stir fries along with mushrooms, red pepper, lots of dill, dry mustard powder and a little sea salt. Or remove seeds, not the skin, grate and freeze for winter baking.

Winter squash includes pumpkin, acorn, butternut, buttercup and spaghetti squashes. Their rich colour means they are high in carotenes, so give protection against some cancers, heart disease, and diabetes. Winter squashes are a good source of vitamin A, B, C and potassium. Spaghetti squash is usually yellow.

Sweet Potatoes are imported in the winter, but a super best buy for nutrition load, especially beta-carotene and vitamin C. They may help prevent cancers, eye disease, depression and heart disease. Easy to use: peel, chop in chunks, boil in a little water, OR bake in oven (takes longer, becomes sweeter). Sweet potatoes are sometimes called "yam", and can be used in place of winter squash in recipes.

Tomatoes (actually a fruit developed by Indigenous farmers in Peru) are said to be "the healthiest of all fruits." But we use them as vegetables, mostly. Tomatoes have the highest concentration of lycopene, an antioxidant proven to stave off cancer, heart disease and other dreaded diseases. Tomatoes are terrific for our blood sugar and our vision and are high in vitamin C, especially in the jelly around the seed (so don't throw the seeds out!). Store at room temperature and not in the fridge as they will get mealy; and do not wash until ready to eat. Cooking and processing actually increase tomatoes' power (as in tomato sauce). Leaving the peel in the brew gives more good fibre, but if you must peel them, drop them into boiling water for one minute, then into cold water. Skin slips off easily. How about a local tomato for breakfast rather than an imported orange? Heirloom tomatoes give a splendour of colours, shapes and luscious tastes, and no taste beats your own tomato just plucked from your own plant – even on a balcony!

Turnip or rutabaga is a winter hero because it is locally available most of the winter (ask your grandparents). Turnip belongs to the same brassica family as cabbage and broccoli, so has the same kind of super benefits, especially the turnip greens. Even the root is good for weight loss (very low calorie), for managing diabetes, and is rich in vitamin C and other powerful antioxidants. Rutabaga is like turnip but more purple and sweeter. Names are interchanged but what we commonly eat is actually rutabaga. Turnips were my husbands' favourite vegetable, but I detested them! Then I began putting a dollop of maple syrup on my portion, and voila, problem solved - we were both happy!

Vegetables that are most heavily sprayed with pesticides (unless organic or non-chemical) are celery, bell peppers, spinach, lettuce, potatoes, cucumbers and kale.

Vegetables that are lowest in pesticides are onions, cabbage, green peas, asparagus, sweet potatoes and mushrooms.

Wild Vegetable Treasures

Eat only if not sprayed.

Chickweed: our gardens are matted with it but take heart! The leaves and stems are higher in iron and zinc than any domesticated green and are also high in potassium and other goodness. Add to salads and soups, steam with other vegetable greens. Pluck only the top 2 inches and wash well.

Dandelions are Nature's super gift to us! Settlers brought dandelions to this continent because they valued the plant as food and medicine. Both dandelion leaves and roots have been used by ancient and modern healers for a host of ailments: as a diuretic; laxative; detoxifier (thanks to slight bitterness); for gout; improving liver, urinary tract, gall bladder and kidney function; reducing high blood pressure; promoting weight loss – and more! Dandelion is considered safe in all quantities. Its golden flower contains "helenin," a chemical compound that may enhance night vision. Use the petals in salads, biscuits, pancakes and dandelion flower syrup.

Dandelion leaves are the queen of greens – the top-most nutritious leafy vegetable. They give more vitamin A and beta-carotene than carrots, more potassium than bananas, more iron and vitamin A than spinach; as well as vitamins C, B, calcium, iron, magnesium, plus, plus, plus. Dandelion greens can be combined with or substituted for other greens in any recipe, such as in lasagna. Snip into soups and stews. Stir-fry or steam like spinach and add onion, garlic and a touch of soy sauce, and save the juice for vegetable stock. For salads, dandelion greens are mighty powerful dark greens, snipped in along with the other ingredients. Saucy dandelion flowers can also be added to salads.

Note that each dandelion leaf grows up from the base, not from along a stalk. Make sure they have not been sprayed, and then wash well. You can cut them with scissors or you can pull the greens off the spine - a bit of bitter is good! If you pick or mow the flowers before they go to seed, you curb spreading. But remember to delight in the springtime glory of a yellow field. That is the first springtime food the bees desperately need. As dandelions are essential for the health of bees, bees are essential for the survival of humans. One-third of our food depends on the pollinating work of bees, but bees are severely threatened, especially by pesticides on the plants they visit. So don't spray the dandelions!

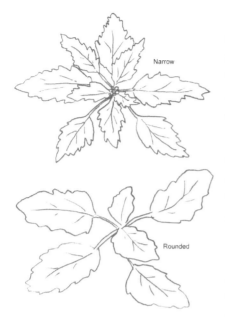

Narrow

Rounded

Lamb's Quarters (Wild Spinach or Pigweed) are among the top-most nutritious of all leafy green vegetables, almost beating dandelions! But we know them as a very common "weed." If you must pull them out, rescue the arrow-shaped leaves and upper stems, with their nice smooth texture and taste; add to spinach or soup. I nurture them as a desired, high nutrition vegetable. Recognize wild spinach by its arrow-shaped leaves and the fine waxy powder on the growing tips. Orache (red spinach) is an edible relative of Lamb's Quarters.

Purslane is a natural growing mulch or ground cover, defamed as a weed, but actually a gift to us. Purslane brings far more Omega-3 and vitamin E than any other green, plus more iron than spinach, and other antioxidants to protect us from the various toxins in our environment – these are the same antioxidants which give the plant its own toughness. Purslane's small leaves and reddish, spreading-out stems are thick with moisture, giving it drought resistance. Purslane is a popular vegetable in the Mediterranean; it grows best in hot, direct sun, but does need some water. Gather the leafy stems and eat in salads and soups, scrambled eggs and smoothies.

Learn More:

The Dandelion Celebration: A Guide to Unexpected Cuisine by Peter Gail

Edible Wild Plants: Wild from Dirt to Plate by John Kallas

Dandelion Medicine: Remedies and Recipes to Detoxify, Nourish, Stimulate by Brigitte Mars

Chapter 10:
More With Less

Eating Well on Little Money
by Pauline Ferland

There is a definite relationship between the loss of a steady income and my interest in eating healthy, low-cost foods. Working less gave me more time to walk to small shops, so I gradually discovered beans, peas, lentils, quinoa, hemp, different kinds of rice and grains, less well-known fruits, vegetables and herbs.

"Doing the Farmers' Market" has become a regular social event. Vendors gladly offer cooking suggestions. Meal preparation is now more labour intensive, but gives a sense of re-connecting with Nature. I am seeing food through completely altered senses.

Charles Long's book How to Survive Without a Salary: Learning How to Live the Conserver Lifestyle inspired me to rethink my strategies – to separate needs from wants. Digging up grass to plant a garden eliminates the need for a lawn mower. Allowing some dandelions to grow provides a source of tea and salads, and saves money for non-negotiables. Experimenting with less oil, sugar and salt gives cheaper, healthier and still tasty food.

I realize that food from the Farmers' Market or Health Food store may seem more expensive than supermarket food. But I know that locally-grown food, especially if chemical-free, is far better value for my health, and Earth's health too. I economize elsewhere, through buying much less so-called "food" that is processed and packaged. Making my own food such as soups, hummus, ketchup, dressings and scones has yielded great savings, and I can actually pronounce the ingredients! I eat less meat but of better quality, more beans and lentils which are cheap when I cook them myself.

My initial choice for Voluntary Simplicity was not entirely voluntary. But even if my financial circumstances changed, I would not want to go back to my old way of eating.

> **Pauline Ferland** tries to make as small a footprint on the Earth as she can, and as large an impact as she can while helping the Earth and Earth's people.

> *"Food – buy it with thought – cook it with care – serve just enough – eat what would spoil – save what will keep – home grown is best"* – posted in Baked Food Cafe, New Glasgow N.S.

Use up Leftovers

Let your fridge give ideas for the meal. Be creative. Add leftovers to stir-fries, scrambled eggs, soups, stews and smoothies.

Try Meat Alternatives

Beans, dry peas, lentils, hemp, quinoa, eggs and fish are less expensive than good quality, local meat. If we eat more of the alternatives, then we can afford to buy a little of the good meat, if we want meat. More and more people are living happily with no meat at all.

Go Gleaning and Sharing

Volunteers pick unwanted fruit to be divided among the fruit picker, the owner, and a food-giving organization. Gleaning Fruit Projects with various names are in many cities across Canada such as Fruit for Thought in Regina and Out of Your Tree in Saskatoon, as well as the Hamilton Fruit Tree Project, the Calgary Urban Harvest Project, Edmonton's Operation Fruit Tree Rescue and Vancouver's Earth Matters Fruit Tree Project. Europe has a network of organized gleaning in farmers' fields after harvest – there is an idea for here! Also, people may willingly let us share some of their unwanted red stem rhubarb, apples or dill weed. People are most happy for us to glean their unsprayed dandelions, leaves and flowers, and become healthy! *The Gleaners and I* is a film about gleaning in Europe.

Buy in Bulk

It is cheaper, with less of the environmental footprint of excess packaging – but only if you can store the extra food and use it all. You can also share the food and the cost with someone else.

Plant a Garden

Grow your own herbs and lettuce, a few tomato plants or a strawberry plant in pots on a balcony or in a sunny spot. Better still, dig a small patch and plant various vegetable seeds or seedlings. Learn from local gardeners what works. Nothing is tastier or healthier – cheap too. Join a community garden to grow your own plot. There, water and other aids are provided as part of the deal and you can become part of a friendly gardening community.

Good Food Boxes

In Regina, register with REACH at 306-347-3224 or visit www.reachinregina.ca. REACH is a community-based program that provides the Good Food Box of fresh food stuffs such as vegetables and fruit at low cost. In Saskatoon contact CHEP (Child Hunger & Education Program) at 306-655-4575 or visit www.chep.org. Search your own community for a similar program, or start one! On the internet visit Food Secure Saskatchewan and Food Secure Canada.

Real Food for Real Needy People

In his book *The Urban Food Revolution*, Peter Ladner reports that studies in Vancouver have shown clearly that regularly feeding the neediest people nourishing food (no white flour and no pop, low sugar, but lots of vegetables and protein) dramatically reduces public spending on police, health services and 911 calls. Dangerous acts are triggered when people are hungry; their systems are out of balance so they have no energy for self-control. Thus feeding people well is a cost-effective crime prevention and drug treatment measure.

"In the far north of Saskatchewan, a nutritious food basket costs almost twice as much as in a large city in the south" says a 2011 report from the Populations Health Unit in Northern Saskatchewan. The price of alcohol is the same at every store in Saskatchewan, but the cost of a 4-litre jug of milk is $16 in northern Saskatchewan; in Regina it is $4 to $5. In Manitoba, the price of milk is the same throughout the province. Consider also that income for northern Aboriginal people is lower than in the south.

Something to think about: What can be done about this food injustice?

Substitutions	
What can I use instead of?	**Substitute**
Wheat flour	Non-gluten flours. Mix 1/3 sweet rice flour (helps hold it together) with quinoa flour, buckwheat flour or chickpea flour to equal the original amount
1 cup (250 mL) wheat flour	7/8 cup (200 mL) gluten free flours such as amaranth, chickpea, buckwheat, quinoa, and rice flours
1 cup (250 mL) wheat flour	3/4 cup (175 mL) millet and oat flours
White flour	Whole grain wheat or rye flour minus 1 Tbsp (15 mL) per cup. Baking will be heavier, but tastier and healthier!
1 tsp (5 mL) baking powder	1/4 tsp (1 mL) baking soda plus 1/2 tsp (2 mL) cream of tartar
1 Tbsp (15 mL) corn starch (avoid GMO)	1 Tbsp (15 mL) arrowroot or tapioca starch (GMO-free, gluten-free and work better than corn starch). Quinoa works as a thickener in soup or stew. Tapioca is an ancient starch made from the root of the cassava or yucca plant native to South America and the West Indies. Arrowroot is made from the underground stem of the tropical arrowroot plant
Bread crumbs	Rolled oats or flakes of quinoa, kamut or spelt
1 cup (250 mL) sugar	3/4 cup (175 mL) maple syrup or honey and 1/4 cup (60 mL) LESS liquid OR 2 Tbsp (30 mL) MORE flour; also reduce oven temperature by 25°F (15°C)
Chocolate or cocoa	Equal amount of carob flour (use less sugar)

1 square (1 oz / 28 gms) chocolate	3 Tbsp (45 mL) cocoa plus 1 Tbsp (15 mL) butter
1/2 cup (125 mL) corn syrup (avoid)	1/3 cup (75 mL) liquid honey
1 cup (250 mL) milk	1 cup (250 mL) water with 1/3 cup (75 mL) dried milk powder (use a blender or an egg beater)
Milk	Goat's milk, hemp beverage, vegetable water or fruit juice
1 cup (250 mL) sour milk or buttermilk	1 cup (250 mL) sweet milk plus 1 Tbsp (15 mL) vinegar or lemon juice. Let sit 5 minutes until curdled
1 cup (250 mL) sour cream	1 cup (250 mL) yogurt or buttermilk
Grated lemon or orange rind	Frozen orange concentrate (replacing part of the liquid)
1 cup (250 mL) stock	1 cup (250 mL) water plus 1 bouillon cube (low sodium), or miso
1 large lemon	1/4 cup (60 mL) bottled lemon juice
1 cup (250 mL) tomato juice	1/2 cup (125 mL) tomato paste plus 1/2 cup (125 mL) water
1 package active dry yeast	1 Tbsp (15 mL) powdered active dry yeast
1 tsp (5 mL) dry mustard powder	1 Tbsp (15 mL) prepared mustard
1 small clove garlic	1/4 tsp (1 mL) garlic powder
1 Tbsp (15 mL) fresh herbs	1 tsp (5 mL) dried herbs
1 Tbsp (15 mL) tamari	1/4 tsp (1 mL) salt
Pine nuts and other exotic nuts	Local hulled hemp seeds, ground flax seeds or sprouted lentils

Chapter 11:
Saving: Storing, Freezing, Drying, Wasting – or Not Wasting

Storing

Use glass, steel, cloth and paper for food storage as much as possible. Read about the real hazards of plastic in food storage in **Chapter 8: Plastics. Sometimes in this world we have to make compromises, balancing one value against another.** We continue to suggest the least harmful types of plastic containers for food storage when necessary. But try to avoid plastics whenever possible. We do the best we can in the situation we are in.

Buy vegetables that are as close as possible to picking time because the nutrients deteriorate.

Storing leafy greens: wash, shake off excess water. Wrap in a small cloth towel and tuck into a plastic bag with end open; large cloth napkins work well. Store greens separately from other vegetables and fruits to protect the greens from ethylene gas which some other produce can emit, hastening the rate of ripening.

Remove purchased vegetables and fruits from plastic bags.

Remove plastic wrap from English cucumbers and plastic wrap covering the berry baskets so they can breathe.

Tomatoes should be left at room temperature. Putting them in the fridge makes them mealy.

Potatoes, squash and sweet potato are best in a cool, dark place in a cloth or paper bag.

If you can't use up bread soon enough, slice and freeze some of it.

A set of fancy plastic bonnets cover bowls handily, without wasting plastic or aluminum wrap.

A non-plastic plate is even better.

If you must use **aluminum** wrap, you can also clean it, fold it carefully, and use again; then recycle it.

Rainforest Relief reports that aluminum is one of the most destructive mining products in the world. Most aluminum ore (bauxite) is in the tropics. First comes destroying the pristine forest, then strip mining leading to soil erosion, pollution of groundwater and air, and destruction of the lives and sustenance of the people, plants and animals. As a displaced farmer in Jamaica said, *"the money is not worth the destruction of the land and the pollution of our air and water."* Then it takes massive energy to create the extreme heat needed to extract the aluminum from the ore, creating massive waste dumps. The heat energy often comes as hydro power from huge dams built on wild rivers, flooding the rainforest. As the flooded wood decomposes underwater without oxygen it creates methane, which is a greenhouse gas 23 times more powerful than CO_2. See www.rainforestrelief.org for more information.

Aluminum is 95% recyclable. If we recycled all present aluminum, and avoided using more (pop cans?) that would discourage companies from more mining and more destruction.

Freezing

Best: store food in a freezer-safe glass jar or glass dish, leaving 1/2 inch free at top to allow for expansion. Remember to take it out of the freezer ahead of time to start thawing.

Plastic: A less dangerous plastic food container is the yogurt-type tub. Hold under warm water a few moments to loosen, so contents can be dumped out to thaw in a non-plastic container.

Plastic freezer bags are handy to make flat packs of lentils or beans in amounts useful for recipes. Be sure to label and date.

Freezing fruits and herbs: wash well and drain, then spread berries, cut fruits or herbs on a cookie sheet (covered with waxed or parchment paper unless the cookie sheet is glass). Place in the freezer until frozen, then into glass jars or flat freezer bags. Label and return to the freezer.

Freezing vegetables: it is best to buy lots in season, local and preferably organic; then freeze or preserve in jars. OR buy frozen: as they are quick-frozen, they are often fresher than "fresh" produce which has travelled a great distance and been in storage.

Wash well, and then blanch by steaming or boiling for 2 to 4 minutes. This inactivates the enzymes that cause deterioration. Drain, spread on a cookie sheet, place in the freezer for 2 to 3 hours, and then put into freezer bags. Sweet peppers and tomatoes are an exception: they do not need to be blanched, just cut in usable sizes and pop into freezer bags.

Freezing soups: Make a big batch, enjoy what you can. Give a jar to an ailing person, invite someone for lunch, or freeze the leftovers for another day, preferably in a wide-mouthed glass jar, or a yogurt-type tub.

Drying

Herbs: Clean well in a bowl of water. Press dry in a cloth towel or a spinner. Lay out on trays to dry at room temperature or tie a string around and hang in an airy spot, not in direct sun. Or if you have a car, on a hot day, lay herbs or teas on trays inside the car, but not in direct sun. That "oven" will do the trick in no time! When thoroughly dried out, store herbs for winter, in glass jars, labelled with date.

A solar food **dehydrator** is a practical way to preserve fresh food's goodness. Using the sun's energy to dry food harkens back through the mists of human pre-history. Today a solar food dehydrator does the same, only faster as the sun's free power reduces the food's water content. The moist air moves off through adjustable air vents regulating air flow and temperature. The internet is loaded with instructions for building your own solar dehydrator.

Wasting – or Not Wasting

Nearly half of all food produced world-wide is wasted, discarded in processing, transport, supermarkets and kitchens, according to the David Suzuki Foundation. Also in the developing world, crops are wasted for lack of safe storage, and transportation to market. In the developed world unused food is thrown to rot in landfills where it becomes a major source of methane gas, a greenhouse gas 23 times more potent than CO_2. This tossed food represents masses of water, fossil fuel energy and human energy used to grow and transport that wasted food.

Composting Made Easy
by Naomi Hunter

Compost is a lovely and free alternative to expensive fertilizers and soil builders. Every year, our vegetables and flowers use up some of the nutrients in the soil so we must build organic matter back into the earth. As well, our landfills are rapidly filling up with "green waste" from people's homes. By composting, we can reduce the trash leaving our house by around 30%.

Compost is any non-animal food waste or organic matter that can rot down to produce soil. We can save compostable material in our home by keeping a little bucket with a lid under or beside the kitchen sink. Add in vegetables, fruit, coffee grounds, tea bags or leaves, grain products, egg shells and paper napkins.

As well as the "green matter" from our kitchen, our compost also needs "brown matter" such as dry leaves, brown paper, dried grass, sawdust, plus soil. I keep a pile or a bag of "browns" beside the outdoor compost box, ready for easy use.

Outside, the compost heap is preferably a wooden box with no bottom which invites the natural soil micro-organisms and earthworms to do their magic work in the composting process.

To start the compost heap, put a several inch layer of brown matter in the bottom of the box and dump a pail of "green" household scraps in the centre. Next cover with "browns" – about double the amount of the "greens." This process will ensure proper nitrogen to carbon mixture and keep the heap from smelling poorly.

When you add your next pail of "green matter," pull back the "browns" and dump the new pail on top of the "greens," then cover with more brown matter. Repeat.

Lastly add water. If it does not rain, water occasionally; compost heaps function best with the consistency of a damp sponge.

Vermicomposting allows apartment dwellers to still compost. Worms can be stored with no smell, in a small "food grade" plastic bin. These delightful creatures efficiently turn your food waste into beautiful soil in a very short time. The book Worms Eat My Garbage by Mary Appelhof is a helpful resource for setting up a worm bucket in your home.

Compost Tea *is literally a "tea" made from fresh food scraps. Fill a large pot with fresh vegetable and fruit scraps. Brew some nice-smelling herbal tea and pour over the vegetable and fruit scraps to fill the pot. Cover and let sit for about a week, then strain out the pulp and toss into your outdoor compost, saving the "tea." This lovely liquid is now a non-toxic fertilizer for houseplants or outdoor plants that need an extra boost – but not for humans!*

Happy growing! If you want more composting suggestions or help, email naomi.ness6@gmail.com.

Naomi Hunter has a master's composting certificate and implements her health and natural living knowledge through all aspects of life. When living in Victoria in a school bus-turned-moving house she helped reclaim waste landscape by soil-building with green waste so impoverished people could grow their own food.

Naomi and her children were the first people living year-round at the Craik Sustainable Living Project. They wintered in a Mongolian Yurt and helped start a community composting project. Now in winters she works as a fitness instructor; in summer she grows all her family's food organically and helps her father with his organic orchard.

Chapter 12:
Action

"Those who have the privilege to know, have the duty to ACT." – Albert Einstein

At Home, I Can

Resolve to continue a journey to eat with justice – to eat food that is healthy for all of us and for the Earth. Give thanks for the wondrous bounty of local harvests.

Resolve to prepare more home-cooked meals.

Before I buy, ask:

   Where did this food come from?
   What did it cost the environment, and the workers?
   Were the animals treated ethically?
   Who profited?

Be aware of food labelling and marketing tricks. Terms like "natural" or "green" do not necessarily mean better. Read the label carefully.

Ask for locally grown produce to be available at my local grocery store.

In season, delight in fresh, tasty foods grown nearby. Shop at the Farmers' Market and come away smiling. It is better when I can reach one without driving too far. Or I can go by bus with a carry-all buggy, or ride-share with a friend.

Get to know my local food producers. Sometimes I can choose local even if not "certified organic," thus supporting the survival of family farms.

Stock up on local produce, learn to freeze or preserve local food to enjoy through the winter. I can even do without, until the treats such as tomatoes, asparagus and strawberries return in season.

Join a Community Supported Agriculture (CSA) program or team up with someone else for a share.

Eat good quality, ethically-raised meat. Try protein alternatives.

Be adventurous – discover and learn how to prepare unfamiliar foods.

When tempted to buy time with quick processed convenience food, I can discover the satisfaction of spending time creating real food, investing in life. Meanwhile, I can share this magic with a child.

Grow food in my own space such as back or front lawn; on a balcony or big pot on the patio. In winter, a sunny window can be a happy spot for some herbs or sprouts.

In the Community, I Can...

Plant fruit or nut trees, or "rescue" neglected fruit. (Search: Urban Food Harvesting in Canada).

At my school or work cafeteria, at community potlucks, faith groups and church suppers I can encourage others to use local, organic and Fair Trade produce.

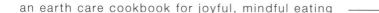

Support locally-owned restaurants that prepare food from local and organic sources, using real plates and cutlery. Bring my own mug or take-out container.

Support local food projects in my community: a community garden, a community kitchen or a "public produce project" which grows food in spare spaces for anyone to nurture and pick.

Work for accessibility to real food for everyone in our society, including those who are poor, disabled, living in "food deserts," lacking transportation or basic information.

Lobby for government support for food production in cities.

Work with education systems to make knowledge about healthy eating, food preparation and food growing essential curriculum at all levels, starting with daycare centres.

Urge provincial and federal support for small organic family farms, balancing the massive support given to conventional agriculture.

Press for federal policies allowing local people in developing countries to control their own food systems, to feed themselves without pressures from Western agribusiness, and without the ravaging of their land and water by Western business projects.

Learn about how food and agriculture and land use critically impact climate change, food security and world peace.

Our world is overwhelmed with poor food policies and choices. Good choices are often hard to find. I can do my best, enjoy the journey toward real food, and be thankful.

> *"Even if I knew that the world would go to pieces, I would still plant my apple tree."* – Martin Luther

Chapter 13:
Recipes

A Blessing

As our great star, the sun graciously shares light,
Warmth and energy with us,
May we as children of the Earth and the sun,
Share with one another the life and joy of this meal.
We acknowledge that the food and drink before us
Is sun-soaked and filled with star energy.
In this food and drink is the taste of the heavens.
May we partake of it in peace with each other
And with all the Earth.

Excerpt from *Prayers for a Planetary Pilgrim* by Edward Hays. Copyright 2008 by Ave Maria Press, P.O. Box 428, Notre Dame, IN 46556. Used with permission of the publisher.

Eating With Justice: giving thanks for the wondrous bounty of local harvests.

The Best Food Practices for all Recipes in *Every Bite*:

Whenever possible:

- Avoid canola oil as it is genetically modified; substitute with camelina oil, extra virgin olive oil or organic sesame oil.
- Avoid all forms of corn (unless organic) because it is all genetically modified. Study the fine print.
- Use organic or pesticide-free local fruits and vegetables whenever possible. Peel non-organic fruit as there is pesticide residue in the rind. Always use organic celery as celery has the highest amount of pesticide residue.
- Source sprouts from a local Farmers' Market or grow your own sprouts.
- Choose local, grass-finished and respectfully–raised meat and free-range eggs and chicken.
- Look for the Fair Trade symbol on packages when shopping for sugar, coffee, tea, chocolate, etc.
- Gently fry spices in very little oil to help essential oils emerge and deepen the flavour. Cook just until the spices smell toasted (any longer and you risk burning them).
- When using dried herbs, crush the leaves before adding them to recipes. This helps to release some of the essential oils and make the herbs more flavourful.
- Grinding flax seeds in a blender or coffee grinder releases the mighty flax goodness.
- Use local honey. When a recipe calls for honey, reduce oven temperature slightly.
- To liquefy honey, place the crystallized honey in a glass jar or steel bowl, and set the jar in hot water.
- Use authentic 100% pure maple syrup, not the "faux" maple

syrup which is made from high-fructose corn syrup.

- Use low-sodium, MSG-free and GF bouillon cubes or miso.
- Tamari sauce can be organic, low-sodium and wheat-free, so is GF. Check the label.
- Save cooking water from vegetables to use for vegetable stock.
- The number of servings is only a suggestion. It all depends on the number and age and appetite of the eaters and on what other food is offered.
- You can skip the beginning sauté stage and in most recipes just add all the ingredients into the mixture without using oil (probably healthier).

In this book, the word "organic" means either free of synthetic chemicals, or "certified organic," with apologies to the farmers who pay the costs and extra work of being "certified."

Feel free to experiment, varying ingredients and amounts, and always give thanks to the Workers, the Creatures, and the Earth.

Listen here to many voices, quotes from the contributors and testers of recipes. They are denoted by quotation marks.

Breakfast Bites: Cereal, Yogurt, Eggs

Breakfast is the most important meal of the day. Greet the day with protein and fibre and lots of water (pop and coffee don't count). Fibre is in food that comes from plants. It provides bulk to keep the bowels healthy, and sweeps out the toxins that could lead to cancer and other ills. Fibre helps lower blood cholesterol levels and regulate blood sugar levels, but note that too much fibre can be problematic. Get fibre from: fruits and vegetables (leave skin on whenever organic or chemical-free); cereals using whole grains; nuts and seeds; and pulses including dry beans, peas, lentils.

Cereal

Porridge MIXTURE (*EASY*)
"This is my favourite. I keep it in a jar and use as needed."

3 cups (750 mL) quick rolled oats (not instant)
1 cup (250 mL) local quinoa
1/2 cup (125 mL) hulled, raw sunflower seeds (not salted)
1/4 cup (60 mL) each: hulled hemp seeds and ground flax seed

Perfect Porridge | Serves 2
1 cup (250 mL) water
1/2 cup (125 mL) Porridge MIXTURE or quick rolled oats
1/2 cup (125 mL) fruit, such as raspberries, cherries, saskatoon berries, haskaps, blueberries, cranberries, chopped or stewed apples or stewed rhubarb

- If using just quick oats instead of MIXTURE add 1 Tbsp (15 mL) hulled hemp seeds and 1 tsp (5 mL) ground flax seed.
- On the stove: into a small pot combine Porridge MIXTURE or rolled oats with water.
- Bring to a boil, turn heat down to gentle boil for 5 minutes. If it sticks a bit, turn the heat off and let stand with cover on for a few minutes to steam loose.
- Add fruit to heat through, without cooking it.
- Serve with milk or hemp beverage or plain yogurt, plus a spoonful of local honey and a sprinkle of cinnamon.

Instant Porridge for the Microwave
"Speedy energy-to-go before rushing off to work!"

- Mix **Perfect Porridge** ingredients in a microwave-safe bowl (use glass, not plastic or metal) and microwave for 3 minutes.

Dry Cereal

- Use only whole grain cereal.

- Read the fine print. Note the amount of sugar/sucrose/fructose/ syrup content, because dry cereals can contain high amounts of extra fattening high fructose which is the worst kind of sugar, and made from GM corn. Also notice if the cereal is whole grain. Are you avoiding milk? Try milk alternatives or a little fruit juice which also adds sweetness.

- To add more nutrition and fibre to packaged dry cereal add a spoonful of raw rolled oats, hulled hemp seeds, ground flax seed, muesli or granola.

- Dry cereals with organic grains are available in Health Food stores.

Muesli (*EASY*)

2 cups (500 mL) large flake rolled oats
1/4 cup (60 mL) sesame seeds
1/4 cup (60 mL) hulled hemp seeds
1/2 cup (125 mL) pumpkin seeds or sunflower seeds
1/2 cup (125 mL) walnuts, washed and chopped, or whatever nuts are on hand
1/2 cup (125 mL) dried cherries, dried cranberries or blueberries

- Mix all ingredients except the fruit and spread thinly on a large pan.

- Bake in the oven at 350°F (175°C) for about 30 minutes. Stir often. Cool thoroughly. Stir in the fruit.

- Store in a glass jar in the fridge.

- Add to other cereal or sprinkle on desserts such as yogurt or applesauce.

Granola

3 cups (750 mL) large flake rolled oats
1 cup (250 mL) spelt flakes or quinoa flakes
1/2 cup (125 mL) mixture of hulled hemp seeds, chia seeds or ground flax seeds

1 1/2 cups (375 mL) mixture of sunflower seeds, pumpkin seeds, sesame seeds, almonds or walnuts (all raw, unsalted)
2 tsp (10 mL) ground cinnamon
1/3 cup (75 mL) camelina oil or sunflower oil
1/3 cup (75 mL) local honey
1 tsp (5 mL) vanilla
1 cup (250 mL) mixture of dried cherries, dried cranberries or dried blueberries

- Mix first 5 dry ingredients in a large bowl.
- Mix the wet ingredients in a small bowl, and then add to the dry mixture.
- Stir all together thoroughly.
- Spread on 2 baking sheets. Bake at 250°F (120°C) for 30 to 40 minutes.
- Stir every 10 minutes. Remove from oven when golden brown and cool thoroughly.
- Add dried fruit. Store in a sealed jar in the fridge.

Buckwheat Pancake MIXTURE
2 cups (500 mL) buckwheat flour
4 cups (1 L) other flour (kamut, spelt, or whole grain wheat)
1 tsp (5 mL) sea salt
5 tsp (25 mL) baking powder

- Mix in a large bowl. Store in a glass jar, ready to use any "pancake morning".
- GF variation: instead of the 4 cups (1 L) wheat flour, use 3 cups (750 mL) quinoa flour (or other GF flour) and 1 cup (250 mL) sweet rice flour (plus the 2 cups (500 mL) GF buckwheat flour).

Buckwheat Pancakes (*EASY*) | Makes 10 pancakes
"They're the best pancakes I ever ate!" – Discerning visitor

1 free-range egg
1 1/4 cup (310 mL) water

1 1/2 cup (375 mL) Buckwheat Pancake MIXTURE

Fruit: 1/2 cup (125 mL) to 1 cup (250 mL) raspberries, cherries, saskatoon berries, blueberries, haskaps or cranberries, fresh or frozen fruit

Camelina oil or sunflower oil as needed to lightly oil the pan.

- In a bowl, beat egg with a fork. Add water, then the Buckwheat Pancake MIXTURE, mixing together only until the dry ingredients are moistened. Add fruit. In a large frying pan on medium heat, spread a little oil.
- Scoop or pour about 1/4 cup (60 mL) batter into the hot pan.
- Watch and turn over as soon as bubbles start to form (about 3 minutes), then flip for another minute or so.
- Serve with yogurt, pure maple syrup, applesauce, stewed rhubarb or organic fruit "topping," which is less sweet than "syrup."
- Freeze left over pancakes. Another day, pop into your toaster and eat like fresh pancakes, or as biscuits, with jam or cheese.

Adapted from the *More-With-Less Cookbook* by Doris Janzen Longacre.

Yogurt

Yogurt Delight (*EASY*)
"An alternative to processed, flavoured, too-sweet yogurt"

Yogurt (plain, live bacterial culture) 1/2 cup (125 mL) for each eater. Fruit such as: raspberries, cherries, saskatoon berries, blueberries, haskaps, cranberries, chopped or stewed apples or stewed rhubarb.

Real maple syrup, local organic fruit topping or liquid local honey. Homemade granola, muesli or hulled hemp seeds.

A taste of grated ginger root (optional).

- Mix fruit and sweetener into the yogurt.
- Top each with muesli or granola, and garnish with a cherry.
- Serve in pretty bowls or glass goblets.

Smoothie Adventures in a Blender (EASY)

A blender (stand-up or hand-held) could be the best useful gift to give a "food challenged" person such as a young person away from home or anyone struggling to eat real food with little money or skill, or no stove.

Fruit Yogurt Smoothie | Serves 1

1/2 cup (125 mL) plain yogurt, live bacterial culture
1/2 cup (125 mL) raspberries, cherries, saskatoon berries, blueberries, haskaps, cranberries, chopped apples and/or other fruit
1 Tbsp (15 mL) hulled hemp seeds
1 tsp (5 mL) ground flax
1/3 cup (75 mL) home-grown sprouts, chopped
1/2 tsp (2 mL) ground cinnamon
1/2 tsp (2 mL) real maple syrup or local fruit topping

- Top up with milk or hemp beverage.
- Whiz in a blender until smooth.

Apple-Dandelion Green Smoothie | Serves 1

1 medium apple, chopped
1 medium pear and/or 1/2 banana, chopped
1/2 cup (125 mL) cherries
1/2 cup (125 mL) cranberries
2 to 3 cups (500 to 750 mL) dandelion greens, chopped
1/2 cup (125 mL) fresh parsley
2 Tbsp (30 mL) hulled hemp seeds
1 cup (250 mL) water

- Mix all together in blender. Whiz until it is smooth as you want.
- Green variations: add chopped leaves of spinach, kale, and/or sprouts.
- Feeling more adventurous? Be Creative!

Create your own smoothie combinations:

- **Fruit (fresh or frozen):** before putting fruit into the blender, chop the hard ones such as pears and apples. Choose from: raspberries, cherries, saskatoon berries, blueberries, haskaps or cranberries.
- **Vegetables:** chopped spinach, kale, dandelion greens, green lettuce, cucumber, carrot, celery, tomatoes, sweet green or red pepper and/or lots of sprouts
- **Flavourings:** mint, ginger root (minced or grated), lemon juice, herbs and/or a touch of cayenne pepper to add some spice
- **Sweeteners:** organic fruit topping, a few drops of real maple syrup or a few chopped dates
- **Extras:** a little peanut or other nut butter, a few cooked lentils and /or raw sunflower seeds
- **Liquid:** yogurt, fruit juice, water, milk, hemp beverage or vegetable stock (with a vegetable smoothie)
- **Health boost:** hulled hemp seeds, ground flax seeds and/or chia seeds.

Eggs

"The only thing that can sit its way to success is a hen."

Eggs: One-a-Day is A-OK! Egg shells are really good to add to the compost, adding calcium to the soil and deterring garden pests. Use free-range eggs when available. **See Chapter 9: Fat, Milk, Eggs.**

Poached Eggs
- In skillet, bring 2 inches of water to a boil. Turn heat down to simmer.

- Carefully crack egg; gently pull shell apart with your thumbs. Drop egg into water.
- Cover. Cook 3 to 5 minutes to desired firmness.

Hard-Boiled Eggs
- Place eggs in a single layer in a pot of cold water, cover with 1 inch of water.
- Bring to a rolling boil over high heat.
- Remove pot from the burner, cover, let sit 15 minutes, and then dunk eggs into really cold water (try ice-cubes). Let eggs stand 1 minute or more, then put back into simmering water for 15 seconds. Immediately crack egg shells gently all over. Carefully peel under cold tap water. Shells will then come off easily.

Deviled Eggs (*EASY)* | Serves 4
4 hard-boiled eggs
2 Tbsp (30 mL) plain yogurt, live bacterial culture
1 Tbsp (15 mL) mayonnaise
1/2 tsp (2 mL) prepared mustard
1/2 tsp (2 mL) ground black pepper
1/2 tsp (2 mL) turmeric
Hot sauce: a few drops to taste
Sprinkle of paprika

- Hard-boil eggs, remove shell, cut eggs in half crosswise, lay on plate.
- Carefully remove yolks.
- Mash yolks in a bowl; add other ingredients (except paprika).
- Stir together and adjust to your taste, then pile into egg-white hollows. Sprinkle paprika on top.

Pickled Eggs: "Cackleberries" | Makes 9
"Handy snack or quick lunch with salad."

9 hard-boiled eggs, shelled
1 1/4 cups (310 mL) apple cider vinegar

1/4 cup (60 mL) water
1 Tbsp (15 mL) local honey
1/2 tsp (2 mL) sea salt (preferably unrefined Celtic sea salt)
2 tsp (10 mL) pickling spice, or 1/4 tsp (1 mL) each: mustard
seed and peppercorns
1 bay leaf
1 chili pepper
1 small garlic clove, minced

- Place eggs in a jar, gently.
- Place other ingredients in a pot, bring to a boil, cool slightly then pour over eggs.
- Cover and refrigerate for 1 week before eating. Keeps safely refrigerated for 3 to 4 months, eggs covered with brine.

Frittata | Serves 4
"Fancy name for easy omelette."

4 free-range eggs
2 tsp (10 mL) camelina oil or extra virgin olive oil
1 medium onion, chopped
1 large garlic clove, minced
1/2 tsp (2 mL) hot pepper, minced (optional)
3 cups (750 mL) fresh greens: use a mixture of chopped local
spinach, dandelion greens, Swiss chard, kale, zucchini or other
vegetables such as tomatoes, mushrooms or peppers
1/2 cup (125 mL) cheddar cheese, grated
1/4 cup (60 mL) fresh parsley or celery leaves, minced, or 1 Tbsp
dried
1/4 tsp (1 mL) sea salt
1/4 tsp (1 mL) black pepper
1/4 tsp (1 mL) basil or thyme

- In a small bowl, beat eggs with a fork or whisk. Add cheese and seasonings. Set aside.
- In a heavy frying pan, sauté the onion, garlic and optional hot pepper in oil until golden.

- Add greens and other vegetables.
- Sauté all for about 10 minutes until soft. Add a few drops of water if needed.
- Pour egg mixture over the vegetables. Cover. Cook over low heat for only a few minutes until egg is set. Take off the heat.
- Serve with local tomato or cucumber slices, or homemade relish.
- Traditional frittata is baked in the oven, which uses more time and energy. Spoon mixture into a lightly oiled 9 inch (23 cm) pie plate and bake in 325°F (160°C) oven for 35 to 40 minutes.

Lunch Bites: Soups, Salads and Dressings

Egg Wraps (*EASY*) | Serves 4

Filling

1/2 cup (125 mL) sprouts
1/2 cup (125 mL) cooked lentils
3 free-range eggs, hard-boiled, chopped
2 tsp (10 mL) onion, minced
2 Tbsp (30 mL) mayonnaise
1 Tbsp (15 mL) plain yogurt (live bacterial culture)
1/4 tsp (1 mL) ground cumin
1/4 tsp (1 mL) ground coriander
Ground black pepper
Prepared mustard to spread

Wraps

- Wraps or tortillas (whole wheat, avoid corn unless organic)
- Mix filling together, except for sprouts.
- Spread wraps thinly with mustard.
- Pile filling into wraps, and add some sprouts.
- Wrap up the goodness and enjoy.

Company Cheesebake (*EASY*) | Serves 6
"Easy for a group lunch; adjust quantities for the number of eaters."

6 slices of whole grain bread
2 1/2 cups (625 mL) cheddar cheese, grated
3 free-range eggs, slightly beaten
2 1/2 cups (625 mL) milk (not skim)
1/2 tsp (2 mL) sea salt
1/2 tsp (2 mL) ground black pepper
1 tsp (5 mL) dry mustard
Hot sauce: a few drops to taste
Optional greens: green onion, parsley, dandelion greens or
spinach, chopped

- Mix together eggs, milk and seasonings.
- In a lightly oiled 9 x 13 inch baking pan place the bread; sprinkle the cheese on top; and then add the optional greens.
- Pour egg mixture over everything.
- Bake in oven 350°F (175°C) about 10 minutes until set.

Curried Egg Salad Sandwiches | Serves 12
12 hard-boiled free-range eggs, peeled, halved
1/4 cup (60 mL) dried local cherries, or currants
1 large green onion, finely chopped
2 tablespoons (30 mL) fresh cilantro, minced
1/2 cup (125 mL) mixture of mayonnaise and plain yogurt (live
bacterial culture)
3 teaspoons (15 mL) curry powder
1/2 tsp (2 mL) sea salt
1/2 tsp (2 mL) ground black pepper
1 small cucumber, cut lengthwise in half
12 slices whole grain bread, lightly toasted

- Put eggs into a large bowl, mash well with fork.
- Mix in cherries or currants, green onion and cilantro.
- Stir in mayonnaise, yogurt, curry powder, salt and pepper.

- Mix in more yogurt, a few spoonfuls if salad is dry.
- Cover and chill. Can be made 3 hours ahead.
- Thinly slice cucumber crosswise into half-rounds.
- Arrange toast on work surface; spread each toast slice with mayonnaise.
- Divide salad among 6 toast slices; top each with cucumber slices and second toast slice.
- Cut sandwiches in half and serve.

Cheesy Bean Tortillas
- Whole grain tortillas or pitas
- Fill with some hummus, sprouts, chopped greens, raw vegetables, grated cheese, puréed beans, pickles, coleslaw or whatever you have that looks good.

Soups

Vegetable Stock
- Save water from boiled vegetables. Save vegetable cast-offs such as the tough part of kale or leaves of celery, unused carrot bits, outer layer of onions, and seeds of pumpkin or squash. Seal in a freezer bag until ready to simmer for soup stock. Strain, then put pulp into compost.
- Create your own soup starting with whatever leftovers and ingredients you have at hand. A blender transforms leftovers. Grab ideas from other recipes.
- Hearty pulse soups can be served as a main dish, with whole grain bread and cheese or hummus.
- Many creamed soup recipes call for a thickening paste of flour or cornstarch. Instead add: quinoa, millet or Red Star nutritional yeast (cheesy flavour, high in vitamin B12) or chopped potato. Avoid any prepackaged thickener with GM corn or soy in it.
- For all recipes, to save time, you can omit the preliminary sauté step and just put everything together in a pot. Probably healthier!

- Serve any soup with a sprinkle of sprouts on top, or a snip of other green herbs. The following recipes are all GF and vegetarian (except the Fish Bulanglang).

Curried Squash or Pumpkin Soup | Serves 6

3 cups (750 mL) butternut or buttercup squash or pumpkin, cooked
1 cup (250 mL) hemp beverage or orange juice
2 1/2 cups (625 mL) vegetable stock or water
2 Tbsp (30 mL) extra virgin olive oil or Better Butter
1/2 cup (125 mL) onion, chopped
1 large garlic clove, minced
5 medium mushrooms, chopped
1/2 tsp (2 mL) ground cumin
1/2 tsp (2 mL) ground coriander
1/2 tsp (2 mL) ground cinnamon
1 tsp (5 mL) curry powder
3/4 tsp (3 mL) ground ginger or ginger root, minced or grated
1/4 tsp (1 mL) dry mustard
1/2 tsp (2 mL) sea salt
Dash of cayenne (optional)

- Peel squash (put seeds in a small pot with water to simmer for vegetable stock, about 30 minutes; dump simmered seeds into your compost bin). Cut squash into chunks; boil gently in the strained stock or a little water until tender.

- Variation: cut squash in half lengthwise and scoop out seeds. Place squash pieces cut side up in a baking tray with 1/2" water. Loosely lay aluminum foil over, to keep squash from becoming dry.

- Variation: puncture squash with a knife in several places and roast whole. Bake at 375°F (190°C) about 45 minutes, depending on thickness, until soft. Cut in half and remove seeds. Scoop out cooked flesh and set aside.

- In large frying pan, sauté together all other ingredients, except the liquid. Add a little water as necessary and simmer for 10 minutes.

- Add the sautéed mixture and all the liquid to the squash; add more liquid as needed.
- Blend just enough to leave some texture (be very careful blending hot soup).
- OR blend only the squash and liquid, before adding to the sauté mixture.
- Serve with a dollop of plain yogurt, chopped toasted organic almonds or sunflower seeds and snips of parsley or chives.

Three Sisters Mexican Squash Soup | Serves 6

The "Three Sisters": corn, beans and squash, have been traditional symbiotic plants of Indigenous farmers from ancient Meso America north to the Six Nations people of Ontario. Growing together, the beans climb up the corn stalk while their roots absorb nitrogen to strengthen the corn. The squash leaves protect the sisters from sun and weeds.

2 cups (500 mL) cooked dry beans.
(To cook, **see Chapter 9: Pulses**)
2 cups (500 mL) winter squash, cooked and mashed
2 cups (500 mL) corn kernels, only local or organic
1 Tbsp (15 mL) butter or extra virgin olive oil
1/2 cup (125 mL) onion chopped
1 garlic clove, minced
1 tsp (5 mL) chili powder
1 tsp (5 mL) ground cumin

2 tsp (10 mL) oregano, dried or fresh
1 tsp (5 mL) sea salt
4 cups (1 L) vegetable stock or water

- Sauté the garlic and onion until golden, then stir in spices and sauté for two more minutes.
- Add squash, drained beans and corn.
- Simmer together for a least 10 minutes to blend flavours and until all vegetables are tender.

Adapted from Sandra Brandt with thanks.

Calling Lakes Lentil Soup with Cranberries | Serves 20

2 cups (500 mL) red lentils
1 large carrot, chopped
1 onion, diced
2 cups (500 mL) diced celery, or lots of celery leaves, chopped or dried
3 cups (750 mL) potato, peeled and diced
8 cups (2 L) vegetable stock, chicken stock or water
1 bay leaf, thyme and other seasonings to taste
Sea salt and pepper to taste
1 cup (250 mL) fresh Canadian cranberries (optional)

- Place washed lentils in a large heavy 12 cup / 3 L pot. Add veggies and seasonings. Bring to boil, and then simmer for 1 to 1 1/2 hours.
- Remove bay leaf. Serve with whole grain biscuits.
- Variation: add 1 cup (250 mL) fresh cranberries for the last 5 minutes of cooking.

Adapted from cook Marlene Naumetz.

Red Lentil Mulligatawny Soup | Serves 8
"Mulligatawny is an Indian soup, not too spicy, easy to make."

6 to 8 cups (1.5 to 2 L) water
1 cup (250 mL) red lentils (not crimson split lentils), washed
1 Tbsp (15 mL) camelina oil or extra virgin olive oil
2 tsp (10 mL) turmeric
1 medium onion, diced
2-4 garlic cloves, minced
2 tsp (10 mL) ginger root, minced or grated
1 large carrot, diced
1 large tomato (fresh local or home frozen), diced
2 1/2 tsp (12 mL) curry powder
1 1/2 tsp (7 mL) ground cumin
1/2 tsp (2 mL) garam masala
1/4 tsp (1 mL) cayenne pepper (or less, to taste)
1 potato, peeled and cubed
1 cup (250 mL) squash or sweet potato, peeled and cubed
1/2 cup (125 mL) dried local organic cherries or raisins
2 small Canadian apples, diced

- In medium pot, combine water and lentils. Simmer 20 minutes.
- In large pot, mix turmeric with oil, then sauté the onion, garlic, ginger and carrot for 3-4 minutes.
- Add tomato and seasonings and sauté for 1 minute more.
- Stir in lentils and cooking liquid, potato and cherries or raisins.
- Cook over medium heat for 20 minutes.
- Stir in apples. Cook 5 minutes more. Serve over local wild rice or millet.

Farmers' Market Vegetable Soup | Serves 6
2 cups (500 mL) small rutabagas ("turnip"), chopped
2 large tomatoes, chopped
2 medium carrots or parsnips, chopped
1 large red potato, chopped
2 medium onions, chopped

5 cups (1.25 L) vegetable stock
1 tsp (5 mL) ground fennel
1/2 tsp (2 mL) ground sage
Any other herbs you fancy
1/2 tsp (2 mL) ground black pepper
Sea salt to taste
1/2 cup (125 mL) local quinoa or kasha (buckwheat groats)
2 cups (500 mL) greens, chopped local spinach, kale, dandelion,
Swiss chard

- Combine all ingredients except greens in a large pot.

- Simmer on the stove for 1/2 hour or in a slow cooker for 8 hours.

- Stir in 2 cups (500 mL) of chopped greens and simmer no longer
  than 5 minutes, just before serving.

Kale - Swiss Chard Bean Soup | Serves 6

1 Tbsp (15 mL) camelina oil or extra virgin olive oil
1 yellow onion, chopped
2 Tbsp (30 mL) garlic cloves, minced
4 cups (1 L) chopped kale leaves (save stem for vegetable stock),
or a large bunch of Swiss chard, or toss in some unsprayed
dandelion greens
6 cups (1.5 L) vegetable stock or water
2 vegetable bouillon cubes
2 tomatoes (fresh in season or home frozen) or 1/2 can of
puréed tomato paste
3 white potatoes, peeled and cubed
2 cups (500 mL) cooked beans (chickpeas, pinto, or whatever
you have) or 2-15 oz cans cannellini (white kidney) or other beans
1 Tbsp (15 mL) seasoning: mixture of oregano, basil, thyme, dill
and sage
2 Tbsp (30 mL) parsley (fresh in season or dried)
Pepper to taste

- Heat the oil in a large soup pot and sauté the onion and garlic until
  golden.

- Stir in the greens and cook until wilted (about 2 minutes).
- Add the water, vegetable bouillon cubes, tomatoes, potatoes, beans, seasoning and parsley.
- Simmer soup on medium heat for 25 minutes, or until potatoes are cooked through.
- Season with pepper to taste (there is already salt in the bouillon).

Quick Do-It-Yourself Creamed Broccoli & Cheese Soup (*EASY*) | Serves 2

1 medium potato, diced
Lots of broccoli flowers and upper stalks (fresh or frozen)
1 inch water
1/2 tsp (2 mL) choice of dried basil, dill, oregano, or celery leaf
Sprinkle of garlic powder
Sprinkle of ground black pepper
Dash of light soy sauce or tamari sauce
1/2 cup (125 mL) mozzarella or cheddar cheese, grated
Milk or hemp beverage for soup consistency

- Boil potato for about 10 minutes until soft, for thickening.
- Add broccoli. Boil gently about 3 minutes, until crisp-tender.
- Set aside some of the broccoli flowers.
- Mix in the seasonings of your choice.
- Turn off heat. Stir in cheese. Add milk or hemp beverage (don't boil).
- Blend together for one minute, or more if you want it smooth, then add the remaining broccoli flowers.
- Optional: substitute cauliflower for broccoli.

Tomato Chickpea Soup | Serves 4

1 Tbsp (15 mL) camelina oil or extra virgin olive oil
1 cup (250 mL) onions, diced
1 cup (250 mL) carrots, diced
2 garlic cloves, minced

1 cup (250 mL) tomatoes (including skins and seeds), chopped

4 cups (1 L) vegetable stock or water (adjust as needed)

1/2 tsp (2 mL) ground black pepper

1/2 tsp (2 mL) oregano (fresh or dried)

1 tsp (5 mL) basil (fresh or dried)

1/2 tsp (2 mL) ground cumin

1/2 tsp (2 mL) celery seed or 1 Tbsp (15 mL) dried celery leaves

1 Tbsp (15 mL) parsley (fresh in season or dried), chopped

1 or 2 cups (250 or 500 mL) cooked chickpeas

- In a soup pot heat the oil, then sauté the carrots, garlic and onions until golden.
- Add all other ingredients. Simmer together until melded. Garnish with chopped sprouts.

Chilled Cucumber Mint Soup | Serves 6
"Cooling on a HOT day."

2 English cucumbers or 5 small, young cucumbers , chopped into chunks, skin on

2 tart apples, peeled and cored, chopped into chunks

1 Tbsp (15 mL) ginger root, minced or grated

20 fresh mint leaves

2 cups (500 mL) plain yogurt (live bacterial culture)

1/2 cup (125 mL) milk, cream or hemp beverage

1 Tbsp (15 mL) lemon juice

1/2 tsp (2 mL) sea salt

- Blend all together until it is as smooth as you want it.
- Set in refrigerator at least 2 hours to chill.
- Serve cold in bowls with snipped onion greens on top.

Best Beanie Borscht | Serves 8

4 to 6 medium size beets

1 Tbsp (15 mL) camelina oil or extra virgin olive oil

1/2 onion, chopped

1 garlic clove, minced

2 carrots, sliced

1 celery stalk plus leaves

2 cups (500 mL) green cabbage, shredded

2 cups (500 mL) kidney beans (cooked) or 1-19 oz can kidney beans, rinsed and drained

3 tomatoes (local, home frozen or canned) or 1/2 cup (125 mL) tomato juice

1/2 tsp (2 mL) ground black pepper or to taste

1/4 cup (60 mL) parsley or dill, minced

2 Tbsp (30 mL) lemon juice or apple cider vinegar

8 cups (2 L) vegetable stock or water mixed with 1 vegetable bouillon cube

- Scrub beets and cut into quarters if large. Boil until they begin to soften. Drain, saving cooking water. Put beets into cold water, then skin slips off easily. Chop into small chunks and set aside.

- In a big pot, sauté the onions, garlic, carrots, celery and cabbage in hot oil until golden, for about 3 minutes.

- Add beets, beet cooking water, tomatoes or tomato juice, beans, herbs, lemon juice or vinegar, pepper, vegetable stock and bouillon cube.

- Bring to boil and then simmer until vegetables are soft enough and melded together.

- Keep tasting and adjust herbs.

- Serve this handsome high nutrition meal with a dollop of plain yogurt, or a sprinkle of feta cheese. Thicker, it is also good as stew.

Adapted from Pulses, Pulse Canada.

Parsnip and Pear Soup | Serves 2
"A delicious, surprising treat."

1 Tbsp (15 mL) camelina oil or extra virgin olive oil

1 large parsnip, peeled, chopped into chunks

1 small onion, chopped

1 garlic clove, minced

1 Tbsp (15 mL) ginger root, minced or grated
1 Tbsp (15 mL) local quinoa
2 cups (500 mL) vegetable stock (more as needed)
1 large fresh Canadian pear, peeled, cored and cubed
1 tsp (5 mL) real maple syrup
1 tsp (5 mL) apple cider vinegar
Garnish with fresh chopped parsley or sprouts

- Sauté the onion, garlic, ginger and parsnip in oil until golden, stirring often for about 5 minutes.
- Add the stock, pears, quinoa, stirring well. Simmer about 15 minutes until all vegetables are soft.
- Blend (be very careful blending hot soup).
- Add maple syrup and vinegar. Garnish with parsley or sprouts.
- Serve in dark bowls for contrast.

Meatless Pea Soup | Serves 12
Peas
3 cups (750 mL) dried peas (split or whole peas from the farmer can be cooked and then blended)

- Wash and soak overnight in about 9 cups (2 L) of water.
- Pour off soaking water. Cover with fresh water, about 9 cups (2 L).
- Add 1 bay leaf. Bring to boil, then simmer for about 2 hours or until peas are soft.

Vegetables
1 cup (250 mL) onion, diced
3 garlic cloves, minced or 2 tsp (10 mL) garlic granules
1 cup (250 mL) celery, chopped or about 1/2 cup (125 mL) celery leaves
2 cups (500 mL) carrots, chopped
1 small potato, peeled and chopped
1 Tbsp (15 mL) camelina oil or extra virgin olive oil
1/2 tsp (2 mL) dry mustard
1 tsp (5 mL) sea salt

1 tsp (5 mL) dried thyme
1 tsp (5 mL) ground black pepper
1/2 cup (125 mL) kale (fresh or frozen), chopped

- In a skillet, sauté the vegetables in oil (except the kale) until golden, stirring often for about 5 minutes.
- Add vegetables to peas along with the seasoning.
- Simmer 10 minutes more, then drop in the kale and simmer for 10 minutes.
- In blender, whiz 30 to 60 seconds only, unless you want it really smooth (be very careful blending hot soup). This soup freezes well in glass jars. Leave space at the top for expansion.

Salads and Dressings

"Pre-packaged organic spring mix of greens is calculated, for each calorie of food energy it provides, to use 57 calories of fossil fuel energy, including growing, chilling, washing, packaging, transporting by refrigerated truck." – Sandra Brandt, based on Michael Pollan

- Make your salads when you're ready to eat them. Fruits and vegetables cut up and left to stand lose vitamins.
- We have **a cornucopia of possible goodies for salads**, so let's create food-art with the following:
- **Dark greens** are the most important; eat every day – green lettuce (not iceberg), spinach, dandelion greens, Swiss chard, parsley, arugula, chickweed, tender beet leaves or kale (kale leaves in winter have travelled far but have loads of nutrients and make salads more leafy green). Celery leaves add a nutritious perk also.
- **Veggies** – tomatoes (local, in season) cucumber, carrots (grated or sticks), beets, fine-cut cabbage (white and red), chives, onions and mushrooms. Pickled beets (home-made or Farmers' Market) add a fancy zing.
- **Tomatoes** – offer a great profusion of varieties, shapes, tastes and colours, thanks to farmers who lovingly nurture heirloom

and other seeds (beyond the common one or two varieties in the supermarket). Tiny tomatoes dress up a salad's party look.

- **Pulses** – lentils, chickpeas and beans.
- Cook a large amount and freeze in small quantities for handy use. To cook, **see Chapter 9: Pulses**.
- **Cheese and eggs** – feta (can be salty so a little goes a long way), local goat cheese, hard-boiled eggs and pickled eggs.
- **Nuts** – raw unsalted walnuts, organic almonds, or sunflower seeds or hulled hemp seeds add a nutrient punch. Most nuts and seeds can be slow dry-roasted in the oven or on the stove top, stirring frequently.
- **Sprouts** – Forget lettuce in the winter, 0-mile sprouts do the trick; buy sprouts from the Farmers' Market or grow your own. **See Chapter 9: Sprouts.**
- **Grains** – cooked quinoa, rice, wild rice, kasha (buckwheat) or non-wheat pasta.
- **Fruit** – raspberries, cherries, saskatoon berries, blueberries, haskaps, raisins, sliced apple, cranberries or cranberry sauce.
- **Edible flowers** – chives, dandelions, nasturtium.
- **Herbs and Spices** – basil, thyme, oregano, dill, cumin, coriander, rosemary, caraway seeds, fresh mint, nasturtium leaves.
- **Dressing of your choice.** Consider adding various herbs and spices, local honey or real maple syrup, or organic fruit topping to your dressings. Commercial Dressings are usually high in sodium (salt) and made of poor quality GMO canola oil, or corn, soy and palm oil.

Basic Dressing | Fits a small (250 mL) jar
1/3 cup (75 mL) apple cider vinegar
2/3 cup (150 mL) camelina oil or extra virgin olive oil or Zatoun olive oil from Palestine (available at Ten Thousand Villages)
1/2 tsp (2 mL) dry mustard
1/2 tsp (2 mL) thyme

1/2 tsp (2 mL) oregano
1/2 tsp (2 mL) basil
1/2 tsp (2 mL) ground cumin (optional)
1/2 tsp (2 mL) ground coriander (optional)
Sea salt and black pepper to taste
Optional: add a little tamari sauce, brown sugar or orange or
lemon juice

- Stir together or shake in a jar. Stir again before each use.

Yogurt Dressing

1 cup (250 mL) plain yogurt (live bacterial culture)
1/4 cup (60 mL) lemon juice
1/4 cup (60 mL) fresh herbs, chopped, such as dill, basil,
oregano, cilantro, mint, parsley and chives
1/4 tsp (1 mL) ground black pepper
Sea salt to taste

- Variation: for a sweet dressing, instead of herbs and pepper add
  organic fruit topping.
- Serve dips with vegetable sticks or rye crisps or GF rice crackers.
  Try to avoid high sodium (salt), GMO wheat crackers.

Winter Purple Salad (*EASY*)
"Handsome!"

Cabbage – green and red (slivered with a knife or coarsely grated)
Sprouts – buy sprouts from the Farmers' Market or grow your
own. **See Chapter 9: Sprouts.**
Pickled beets, chopped
Kale, chopped
Feta or goat cheese, crumbled
Dried cranberries or cherries or raisins
Optional boiled or pickled egg
OR whatever you have on hand

- Make basic oil and vinegar dressing; add a splash of organic
  cherry topping.

Early Spring Prairie Salad
Lentil Rice Mixture
2 cups (500 mL) mixed raw lentils and/or wild rice, cooked on low heat in 4 cups (1 L) water, about 40 minutes or until soft.

• Drain and cool. Save water for vegetable stock.

Vegetable Mixture
Chives from the garden or onions, slivered
Cucumber and tomato from greenhouse, chopped
Sprouts
Dandelion greens (chemical-free), chopped
Feta cheese, crumbled
Anything else that is peeping up

• To the vegetable mixture, add as much of the lentil rice mixture as you want, saving the surplus for another day.
• Combine with dressing of your choice.

Sprinkle with Robin-song – fling open the window and listen!

Broccoli Crunch Salad (*EASY*)
"This is a sure hit with visitors, and easy to put together."

1 head broccoli, cut into bite-size pieces
3/4 cup (175 mL) dried organic cherries, cranberries or raisins
1/2 cup (125 mL) raw sunflower seeds
1/2 cup (125 mL) white, red or green onions, minced
Optional: wild rice (cooked), sprouts or chopped red sweet pepper

- To enhance the flavour, toast nuts and seeds by spreading on a dry skillet on the stove top on medium heat and shuffle around until brown, or spread out in a pan in a medium oven for 3 to 4 minutes.
- Mix together with dressing (below).

Creamy Dressing
1/2 cup (125 mL) mayonnaise
1/2 cup (125 mL) yogurt (plain, live bacterial culture)
1 Tbsp (15 mL) liquid local honey or fruit topping (cherry or saskatoon berry)
1 Tbsp (15 mL) white vinegar

- Whisk together ingredients or shake in a jar.

**Japanese Quinoa Salad | **Serves 10
Combine:
3 cups (750 mL) cooked local quinoa, from 1 1/2 cups (375 mL) dry grain. (To cook, **see Chapter 9: Grains**)
3 green onions, sliced
1/4 cup (60 mL) celery, sliced
3/4 cup (175 mL) cabbage, chopped
1/2 cup (250 mL) mushrooms, sliced
1/4 cup (60 mL) organic almond pieces, toasted
3 Tbsp (45 mL) sesame seeds, toasted

Dressing
1/4 cup (60 mL) sesame oil
3 Tbsp (45 mL) tamari sauce
2 Tbsp (30 mL) lemon juice
2 tsp (10 mL) local honey
1 tsp (5 mL) ginger root, minced or grated

- Whisk together ingredients or shake in a jar.
- Mix dressing into quinoa mixture.
- Let sit for a while to marinate.

Bean Plus Salad (*EASY*)

Combine:

1 cup each (250 mL): black beans and chickpeas cooked (or combination of other pulses)

1/2 medium onion, minced

1 cup (250 mL) cooked wild rice or millet

Fresh local farm vegetables chopped (whatever you have, as much as you want)

Citrus Dressing

1/4 cup (60 mL) lime or lemon juice, or apple cider vinegar

1/3 cup (75 mL) camelina oil or extra virgin olive oil

1/2 tsp (2 mL) black pepper

1/2 tsp (2 mL) garlic powder

1/2 tsp (2 mL) cumin powder

Tiny tomatoes (cut in half, artfully arranged on top)

- Whisk together ingredients or shake in a jar.
- Let sit for a while to marinate before serving.
- Keeps for several days in the fridge.

Fusion Quinoa / Lentil Salad Bowl

Contributed by a super busy critical care nurse. "This is a meal for many occasions. It is my fallback when I want to whip up something filling and tasty. It can also be a pretty dish for dinner guests. I most often make it to bring to my work at the hospital. I cook up the quinoa / lentil mixture and assemble the salad in separate to-go containers the night or day before my stretch of shifts. The quinoa / lentils keep very well and heat up wonderfully, if desired. This salad bowl is delicious and can keep me going for hours! I usually just wing it with any ingredients I have, so use your imagination."

Quinoa / Lentil Mixture

1/2 cup (125 mL) onion (Spanish or white), minced
1 garlic clove, minced
1 Tbsp (15 mL) extra virgin olive oil
1 tsp (5 mL) ground cumin (optional)
1/2 tsp (2 mL) ground coriander (optional)
1/2 tsp (2 mL) cayenne pepper (optional, to taste)
1/2 tsp (2 mL) sea salt
1 tsp (5 mL) ground black pepper (or more to taste)
1 cup (250 mL) local quinoa
1 cup (250 mL) small lentils
3 cups (750 mL) vegetable stock or water

- Heat the olive oil in a deep pot on medium heat.
- Sauté the onion and garlic on low to medium heat until the onions are golden (add a couple of teaspoons of water to deglaze pan if the onions get too browned).
- Add spices, quinoa, and lentils; fry for a couple minutes while stirring constantly.
- Next add water and bring to a boil while stirring occasionally.
- Decrease heat to medium low, cover, and allow mixture to simmer for 15-20 minutes or until fluffy and liquid is evaporated.

Salad Mixture

- Prepare salad mixture with ingredients such as kale, spinach, Swiss chard, cabbage, parsley, basil, chives, sprouts, diced local tomatoes, diced cucumbers, nuts of any variety and goat cheese.
- Serve salad into individual bowls, top with quinoa and lentil mixture.
- Optional: top it off with a fried or poached egg, and hot sauce.

Greek Lentil Salad for a Crowd | Serves 10
"Well received at a meeting."

1 cup (250 mL) green lentils (any variety)
3 cups (750 mL) water
1 bay leaf
1 cup (250 mL) cucumber, chopped
1/2 cup (125 mL) onion, chopped
2 medium tomatoes, chopped
1/2 large sweet yellow pepper, chopped
1 cup (250 mL) cauliflower, chopped
1/2 cup (125 mL) fresh parsley, minced
4 oz (125 mL) feta cheese, crumbled
1/2 cup (125 mL) black olives, sliced

- Rinse and drain lentils.
- In a saucepan, combine lentils, water and bay leaf.
- Bring to boil, cover, and reduce to simmer for 15 minutes. Drain.
- Remove bay leaf. Cool.
- Combine lentils and remaining salad ingredients.

Greek Salad Dressing
Juice of 1/2 lemon
1/2 tsp (2 mL) grated lemon peel
1 Tbsp (15 mL) red wine vinegar
2 garlic cloves, minced
1/2 tsp (2 mL) sugar (Fair Trade)
2 tsp (10 mL) oregano, fresh or dried
1/2 tsp (2 mL) basil, fresh or dried
1/2 tsp (2 mL) mint, fresh or dried
1 tsp (5 mL) Greek seasoning
1/3 cup (75 mL) extra virgin olive oil

- In a blender or by stirring well, combine all dressing ingredients and toss with salad. Chill for several hours or overnight.
- Chill for several hours or overnight.

Extra Bites: Spreads, Sauces, Dips

Spreads

Jam: search for locally made jam in stores. Read the fine print! By law "jam" must contain 66% sugar. But organic sweet fruit spreads like the Over the Hill Cherry Spread have only 30% sugar so must be called "**spreads.**" Their fruit syrup must be called "fruit topping." Spreads and toppings, with less sugar, have shorter shelf life, so must be refrigerated.

Better Butter
A combination of butter and oil is always easy to spread and healthier for you. Butter or margarine? Just look at what is in them! **See Chapter 9: Fat Milk, Eggs**.

1 cup (250 mL) butter (1/2 brick)
2/3 cup (150 mL) camelina oil or extra virgin olive oil

- Leave butter at room temperature until soft, and then slice into small cubes.
- In blender, whiz together butter and oil until smooth. Refrigerate.

Hummus
3 cups (750 mL) cooked chickpeas (To cook, **see Chapter 9: Pulses**)
1/3 cup (75 mL) chickpea juice, from cooking
3 garlic cloves, minced
Dash of tamari sauce
Juice from 1 or 2 lemons
3/4 cup (175 mL) tahini (sesame butter)
1/4 cup (60 mL) chopped sprouts or packed parsley, finely minced, fresh in season or frozen
1 tsp (5 mL) ground cumin
1 tsp (5 mL) ground black pepper to taste

- Mash thoroughly or whiz in a blender. Stop the motion often, and punch down with a spoon.
- If it is still a bit chunky, that's O.K. Store in small glass jars, freeze all but one to use right away.
- Spread on crackers, or pile on a sandwich with sprouts, greens or herbs such as cilantro, home-grown or from Farmers' Market. Thin with a bit of plain yogurt and serve as a vegetable dip.

Adapted from *Moosewood Cookbook* by Mollie Karzen.

Sauces

Pesto
Basil provides a big dose of antioxidants, helps with reducing inflammation and improves memory and mental clarity.

2 cups (500 mL) chopped fresh basil leaves, packed, or chopped dandelion greens, or a mixture of both
1/2 cup (125 mL) grated parmesan or other cheese
1/2 cup (125 mL) camelina oil or extra virgin olive oil
1/3 cup (75 mL) walnuts, rinsed and chopped, or sprouts
2 garlic cloves, minced
1/8 tsp (.5 mL) sea salt
1/8 tsp (.5 mL) ground black pepper

- Combine ingredients in a blender and pulse. From time to time, push down with a spoon; add a wee bit more oil if necessary.
- Serve with pasta, pizza, over potatoes or as a dip.
- Pesto can be frozen; leave out the cheese if freezing.

Pesto with Basil, Swiss Chard and Hulled Hemp Seeds
"I'm better at growing Swiss chard than basil. This pesto makes the most of my modest fresh basil crop and uses all local ingredients. I freeze my pesto in muffin tins, take out one or two to thaw, then toss with hot pasta (try varieties other than white wheat pasta). Garnish with grated Parmesan cheese, or try to find local cheese."

1/2 cup (125 mL) fresh basil leaves
1/2 cup (125 mL) chopped Swiss chard, stems removed
1/4 cup (60 mL) hulled hemp seeds
1/2 cup (125 mL) camelina oil or extra virgin olive oil
A pinch of sea salt

• Blend together until smooth.

Raita
"Cool and quick."

1 cup (250 mL) plain yogurt, live bacterial culture
1 small cucumber or 6 inch English cucumber, minced or grated.
If you are fussy, you can remove the seed centre before grating,
but why waste that good stuff?
1/4 tsp (1 mL) ground cumin or crumbled tarragon
Grated carrot, chopped cilantro (optional)

• Mix together. Goes well with spicy food.

Tomato Sauce or Salsa
For sauce use 12 to 15 medium local tomatoes, including skin and
seeds chopped.

For salsa use about 8 tomatoes.

1 cup (250 mL) celery and leaves, chopped
2 bay leaves (remove at the end of cooking)
3 Tbsp (45 mL) fresh parsley, chopped
1 1/2 Tbsp (22 mL) garlic powder or 2 garlic cloves, minced
1 Tbsp (15 mL) sea salt
1 1/2 tsp (7 mL) ground black pepper
1/4 tsp (1 mL) cayenne, or to taste
1 Tbsp (15 mL) paprika
2 tsp (10 mL) turmeric
2 Tbsp (30 mL) dried basil or lots of fresh basil leaves, chopped
fine
1 tsp (5 mL) oregano

2 Tbsp (30 mL) chives, chopped fine

1 can of pure tomato paste

2 Tbsp (30 mL) local quinoa, for thickening

- Add all ingredients to a large pot, bring to boil, then simmer on stove top. Stir often. When all ingredients are soft, whiz in a blender to make chunks as small as you want them.

- Or place pot in oven at 325°F (160°C). Cover and stir every half hour until ready; or place in slow cooker overnight.

- Save in serving size jars leaving 1/2 inch clearance. Store in freezer.

Rhubarb Tomato Relish | Fills 12 small (250 mL) jars.
"A handy way to perk up most dishes"

6 cups (1.5 L) rhubarb, diced

4 cups (1 L) onion, chopped

1 1/2 cups (375 mL) celery, diced

3 1/2 cups (875 mL) tomatoes, chopped. Use fresh in season, home frozen or 28 oz (875 mL) cans.

2 cups (500 mL) sugar (Fair Trade) or 1 cup (250 mL) sugar and 1/2 cup (125 mL) local honey

2 cups (500 mL) vinegar, white or apple cider

1 tsp (5 mL) ground cinnamon

1 tsp (5 mL) ground cloves

1 tsp (5 mL) sea salt

1 tsp (5 mL) ground black pepper

1 tsp (5 mL) mixed pickling spices, tied in square of thin cotton

- Measure all ingredients into large pot and bring to a boil over medium heat.

- Simmer, uncovered, 35 minutes, stirring often. Discard spice bag.

- Store in small jars, leaving 1/2 inch at the top to allow for expansion. Label and freeze.

- To preserve: reheat ingredients to boiling. Pour into sterilized jars. Tighten lids and metal bands securely. Process in boiling water bath for 10 minutes. Store on shelf.

- Pickling spice seems expensive for using so little of the bag, so maybe share with a friend.

Search for locally made sauces.

Dips

Saskatchewan Goat Cheese Dip

- Mix plain yogurt into herb or spicy pepper goat cheese (or add your own herbs) until it is the right consistency.

Dandelion Dip

"It is good!"

1 cup (250 mL) dandelion greens, chopped
1/2 cup (125 mL) cottage cheese or plain yogurt. Use live bacterial culture, at least 2%.
1/4 cup (60 mL) toasted walnuts or sunflower seeds
2 Tbsp (30 mL) mayonnaise
Optional: 1 tsp (5 mL) prepared mustard

- Purée all together in blender.

Spinach, White Bean and Parmesan Dip

1 cup (250 mL) white beans, cooked and drained
1 cup (250 mL) spinach or mix with dandelion greens, cooked and drained
1 large garlic clove, minced
1 Tbsp (15 mL) camelina oil or extra virgin olive oil
3 Tbsp (45 mL) Parmesan cheese, grated

- Purée all together in blender.

Snack Bites (all EASY)

Almonds (organic) - rinse in a sieve with cool water. Spread out in pan and bake in oven at 250°F (120°C) for 1 hour until crunchy. Check sometimes, and stir. Cool. Mix with dried organic cherries or dried cranberries.

Cucumber Slices - spread with local goat cheese or hummus.

Celery Sticks - stuff with cheese or hummus or nut butter. Line up raisins, dried cherries or cranberries to make "ants on a log." Remember that non-organic celery carries the most chemicals of all vegetables, so eat organic.

Veggie Munch - snap peas, beets, turnips, cucumber sticks or carrots (avoid processed "baby carrots"), pieces of broccoli, cauliflower or fruit. To keep cut apples or peaches from browning while waiting, drizzle with a few drops of lemon.

Tiny Tomatoes - nothing is yummier than our own fresh-plucked tomatoes from a pot on our balcony or a sunny corner in our yard (a pot can be moved around to follow the sun). Don't wash until ready to use. Store at room temperature, as the cold damages them. Look for heirloom tomatoes at the Farmers' Market.

Mushrooms (chemical-free) - wipe with a damp cloth, do not soak in water – they absorb water like a sponge.

French No-Fries
Oven-baked (these are fine without oil)

4 medium potatoes, cut into 1/2 inch wide strips
1 Tbsp (15 mL) extra virgin olive oil (optional)
1/2 tsp (2 mL) ground black pepper
1/4 tsp (1 mL) sea salt
1/4 tsp (1 mL) paprika or chili powder
Parmesan cheese, grated (optional)

- Toss potatoes into a bowl along with the other ingredients. Mix well and spread on a baking sheet.
- Bake at 475°F (240°C) for 20 to 25 minutes or until golden, stirring occasionally.

Kale Chips
Whole, fresh, local kale
1 Tbsp (15 mL) camelina oil or extra virgin olive oil
Herbs of your choice (oregano, thyme, paprika, dry mustard, garlic powder, ground cumin, sea salt and black pepper)
Parmesan cheese, grated (optional)

- Wash kale and remove the centre spine (save in freezer bag for vegetable stock).
- Chop greens into bite-size pieces; pass through spinner to remove excess moisture.
- Put kale into a large bowl. Toss with oil, herbs and cheese until evenly distributed. Toss again.
- Spread a thin layer on a cookie sheet.
- Put into a 350°F (175°C) oven for 10 to 12 minutes.
- When cool, store in a glass jar for nibbling.

Sprout Balls
To grow sprouts, **see Chapter 9: Sprouts.**

- Mix chopped lentil sprouts with local quick rolled oats, a bit of local honey, peanut butter or other nut butter.
- Press into a long roll and leave in freezer for a few hours.
- Slice or roll into balls.

Chickpea Snackers
"Neat! This is good!" – Surprised visitors.

4 1/2 cups (1 L) cooked chickpeas or 2 – 19 oz (540 mL) cans of chickpeas
3 Tbsp (45 mL) extra virgin olive oil

Lots of spices, such as Cajun powder, curry powder, garlic powder, paprika, ground cumin, cayenne or herbs, such as basil, thyme, to taste

- Combine all ingredients in a medium bowl, and then spread on a cookie sheet.
- Bake for 40 minutes in 350°F (175°C) oven.
- Stir often toward the end. Cool. KEEP IN FRIDGE uncovered.

Beet Crisps
4 medium beets
1 Tbsp (15 mL) extra virgin olive oil
Salt, pepper or herbs

- If beet skins are smooth, there is no need to peel them, but scrub well.
- Slice beets very thin.
- In a bowl toss beet slices in oil.
- Lay the slices flat on a baking sheet, in a single layer.
- Bake 30 minutes at 250°F (120°C)
- After the first 15 minutes, turn the beets over. If you have a wire rack to fit over the baking sheet, the beets can be laid on this rack, so do not need to be turned over.
- Cool. Store in an airtight container.
- The same process makes sweet potato, eggplant or zucchini crisps.

Apple Chips
Organic apples
Cinnamon or nutmeg

- Leave skin on the apples. Dig out the core if you wish. Slice apples very thin.
- Lay out in a single layer on a parchment-lined baking sheet or a glass pan, thinly oiled.

- Bake at 225°F (110°C) for 30 minutes. Turn apples over, sprinkle with cinnamon or nutmeg; bake cored apples for another 30 minutes; bake not-cored apples for 1 hour. Cool. Store in an air-tight container.

Popcorn

- Beware! Movie popcorn holds colossal amounts of calories and salt. Let's bring our own snacks! Make organic popcorn (not GM) in an air-popper machine, and then add extra virgin olive oil and sea salt.

- Optional: add coconut oil, cayenne, nutritional yeast, parmesan cheese, paprika, ground cumin, parsley or dill – use your imagination!

Quick Vegetable Drink (or hot soup)

2 cups (500 mL) vegetable stock
5.5 fl. oz (156 mL) can of pure tomato paste
Half a can of "nothing added" tomatoes
1/2 cup (125 mL) sprouts
1/2 cup (125 mL) fresh local greens, chopped
1 Tbsp (15 mL) hulled hemp seeds
1/4 tsp (2 mL) garlic powder
Smidge of cayenne (careful – it's hot!)
1 tsp (5 mL) dried herbs, choice of basil, dill, thyme, oregano, cilantro, celery leaves

- Optional for soup: add 1/2 cup (125 mL) cooked chickpeas or black beans, after blending.

- Experiment with ingredients, depending on what you have.

- Blend until it is as smooth as you want it.

- This is great as a cold drink on a hot day or hot soup on a cold day.

Main Bites: Vegetables, Pulses, Fish, Meat

Vegetables

"Eat food … mostly plants …not too much" – Michael Pollan

- **Stir-fry** - drop a bit of oil into a medium-hot pan, then add the ingredients. Stir for a few minutes, then add a dash of water. Cover and steam until ready.

- **Steam** in a steamer or in just enough water so they don't burn. As soon as they are soft enough sprinkle with a little camelina oil or extra virgin olive oil or Better Butter and whatever herbs or spices you want, such as dill, basil, garlic granules.

Sweet Potato and Dandelion Medley | Serves 4

2 tsp (10 mL) camelina oil or extra virgin olive oil
1 small onion, sliced
1 garlic clove, minced
1 inch (3 cm) ginger root, minced or grated
1 large sweet potato, peeled and sliced very thin
A pile of dandelion greens (well washed), cut in bite-size pieces
A little water to keep from burning, starting with 1/4 cup (60 mL)
A dash of tamari sauce
1/2 tsp (2 mL) dried thyme
1/4 tsp (1 mL) ground black pepper

- Heat oil on medium heat and sauté the onion, garlic and ginger until golden.
- Add sweet potato slices and dandelion greens.
- Simmer in a small amount of water until sweet potatoes are soft.

- Drain and save any liquid for vegetable stock.
- Season to taste.

Dandelion Feta Potatoes
Serves as many as you prepare for.

- Cut local potatoes into quarters.
- Boil in just enough water.
- Add a pile of tender dandelion greens (well washed and chopped) to the potatoes.
- Boil gently until ingredients are soft, then mash together.
- Add black pepper, thyme or dill to taste.
- Add crumbled feta cheese on top.

Dandelion Avocado Sandwich | Makes 2 sandwiches
"Yummy and loaded with health-giving nutrients."

4 slices of whole grain bread
Prepared mustard
1 avocado (organic, just the right ripeness)
Dandelion greens (well washed, coarse spine removed)

- Spread the mustard on slices of bread. Cut avocado in strips and lay on the bread. Pile on dandelion greens, then add the second slice of bread.

Squash

If a squash skin is too hard to cut, heat the whole squash in the oven at 350°F (175°C) for about 20 minutes to soften.

• For all squash and pumpkin seeds, put in a pot with water, simmer for 20 minutes or more and then strain. Save for vegetable stock.

• All of the following squash skins are tender enough to be eaten when cooked (more fibre), or scoop out the flesh and put the skin into the compost.

Spaghetti Squash

"Very tasty with an interesting texture and can take the place of potato in a meal."

• Cut squash in half lengthwise and clean out seeds.

• Place both halves face down in shallow baking pan with 1/2 inch water.

• Bake at 350°F (175°C) for 45 minutes to 1 hour until squash is soft. Scoop the flesh into a bowl and add:

1/4 tsp (1 mL) sea salt
1/4 tsp (1 mL) pepper
1 Tbsp (15 mL) extra virgin olive oil
1 tsp (5 mL) paprika

• Stir very gently so as to preserve, and fluff up the spaghetti-like strings.

• Sprinkle Parmesan cheese on top.

Acorn Squash

- Dark green and shaped like an acorn.
- Cut in half, scrape out seeds and place face up (skin side down) in a pan with 1/2 inch of water. To each hollow add some butter, a pinch of pepper, herbs (especially rosemary) or a drip of local honey.
- Bake about 20 minutes until soft, or steam in a pot on stove top with 1 inch of water and simmer until soft.
- Eat the whole thing, shell and all, if you want.

Buttercup Squash

- Dark green like a flattened ball with sweet orange flesh which is perfect for soup.
- Cut in quarters and remove seeds.
- Bake in oven as for acorn squash at 350°F (175°C) for 45 minutes to 1 hour; or steam on stove-top as for acorn squash.
- Eat directly out of the shell, or scoop flesh out into a bowl and mash, adding seasoning as desired.

Butternut squash

- Yellow skin that is easily peeled, and the long neck is solid flesh.
- Cut across to get circles.
- Chop into chunks, steam in a very little water along with a pinch of rosemary (optional).
- Drain, mash with butter, sea salt and pepper.
- Save cooking water for vegetable stock.

Patapan

- Bright yellow circle, small and frilly, nice cut up in salads.

Curried Fruit Stuffed Squash | Serves 4

1 whole squash (buttercup or butternut)
2 Tbsp (30 mL) butter
1/4 cup (60 mL) onion, minced
2 tsp (10 mL) curry powder
1/4 tsp (1 mL) ground cinnamon
1/4 tsp (1 mL) ground ginger
1/4 tsp (1 mL) sea salt
1 large Canadian apple or pear, chopped
1/2 cup (125 mL) dried organic cherries
1 tsp (5 mL) grated lemon rind
1 Tbsp (15 mL) local honey
Optional: toasted chopped nuts, sesame seeds or raisins

- Soak dried cherries for 10 minutes. Drain. Save soaking water.

- Cut squash in half (buttercup crosswise, butternut lengthwise).

- Bake in oven at 350°F (175°C), cut-side down, until nearly done (about 30 minutes).

- Score the squash flesh into squares. Spread honey and 1 Tbsp (15 mL) butter over the flesh; then add a sprinkle of sea salt and lemon juice. Set aside.

- Meanwhile, sauté onion in 1 Tbsp (15 mL) butter until golden.

- Add chopped fruit, cherries, spices and lemon rind and sauté.

- Stuff fruit filling into prepared squash hollows. Sprinkle with chopped nuts or sesame seeds if you wish. Continue baking until squash is done, another 30 minutes or so.

With thanks to Sandra Brandt.

Buttercup Squash or Sweet Potato, Carrot, Parsnip, Turnip and White Potato Smash

- Peel and boil vegetables in a little water until tender.

- Mash with a dollop of yogurt and herbs.

- Bake in a casserole dish at 350°F (175°C) for about 20 minutes.

Sweet Potato-Carrot-Apple Medley (*EASY*) | Serves 8
"Quick and easy to take to potlucks."

3 medium sweet potatoes, peeled and cubed
4 medium carrots, pared and cut into bite-size chunks
Water (about 1 inch)
2 apples, cored and cubed
1/4 cup (60 mL) orange juice or 2 Tbsp (30 mL) orange juice concentrate
2 Tbsp (30 mL) butter
1 Tbsp (15 mL) local honey
1/4 tsp (1 mL) ground cinnamon
1/4 tsp (1 mL) ground nutmeg

- In large pot, gently boil carrots and sweet potatoes about 10 minutes until just tender-crisp.
- Drain. Save water for vegetable stock.
- Add apples, orange juice, butter, honey, cinnamon and nutmeg.
- Cook barely 5 minutes or until apples are tender but still crisp, stirring often.

Roasted Vegetables
Most veggies can be savoured this way.

Try some: potatoes, carrots, beets, parsnips, onions, squash, zucchini, sweet peppers, mild chili peppers, eggplant, mushrooms, fennel bulbs and whole garlic cloves.

1 tsp (5 mL) to 1 Tbsp (15 mL) extra virgin olive oil (optional)
Fresh basil leaves, chopped
Sprigs of fresh thyme, chopped
Fresh cilantro, chopped
Fresh oregano, chopped
1 Tbsp (15 mL) garlic powder
1/2 tsp (2 mL) to 1 tsp (5 mL) ground black pepper
1/4 tsp (1 mL) sea salt

- Wash / scrub vegetables.
- Cut into bite size pieces and put into a mixing bowl.
- Mix all other ingredients and toss with the vegetables until coated.
- Spread in a thin layer on a baking sheet and bake at 375°F (190°C) for 20 minutes (a toaster oven is great for this).
- Serve over wild rice or millet, whole grain pasta or with beans.

Madeleine's Red Cabbage

"Madeleine was one of the most amazing cooks! She loved to make dishes from her Yugoslavian heritage for her friends and family. She preferred fresh garden produce when it was available so she was always thrilled when I brought her a basket of vegetables from my garden. A sumptuous meal would follow!"

1 red cabbage, chopped
1 small onion, chopped
1 Tbsp (15 mL) extra virgin olive oil
1 cup (250 mL) cranberry juice or water
1 Tbsp (15 mL) local honey
2 Tbsp (30 mL) apple cider vinegar
5 whole cloves
1/4 tsp (1 mL) ground cinnamon
1-2 bay leaves
1 Canadian apple, cut in cubes (optional)

- In a medium pot, sauté the onion in oil until golden.
- Add cabbage, onion and other ingredients.
- Add liquid and boil gently until cabbage is tender.
- Optional: add apple for the last 10 minutes so it remains crisp.
- Remove bay leaves.
- To prevent red cabbage from changing colour to grey, add something acidic like vinegar or lemon juice. Red cabbage has 15 times the beta-carotene of green cabbage.

Kale or Swiss Chard with Dandelion Greens

• Chop greens.

• Chop green onions, red pepper, carrot, zucchini, dandelion greens, kale or Swiss chard and lots of garllc.

• Sauté vegetables and garlic in 1 Tbsp (15 mL) extra virgin olive oil, adding greens last.

• Then add a little water, pepper, lots of dill, and a dash of tamari sauce.

• Cover and simmer until greens are tender, about 5 minutes

• VARIATION: make it hot and spicy with 1 Tbsp (15 mL) paprika, 1/2 Tbsp (7 mL) ground cumin, 1/2 tsp (2 mL) sea salt and a dash of hot sauce.

• VARIATION: make this into a frittata: drain off any liquid, cover with slightly beaten eggs, and add herbs or grated cheese. Cover for a few minutes until eggs are set and serve at once.

Frozen Kale

• Save that super summer farm kale and enjoy its health boost in the winter.

• Get kale fresh from the farm for the most nutrients.

• Remove the tough part of spine and save it in the freezer for making stock. Wash kale leaves and chop. Steam/cook in boiling water for 2 minutes.

• Drain and transfer to ice water for 2 minutes, spin in a salad spinner and lay on a towel and gently squeeze out the remaining water.

• Spread kale over a sheet of parchment or waxed paper on a cookie sheet.

• Leave in the freezer for at least 30 minutes.

• Separate the kale, put in freezer bags, ready for adding to dishes as needed.

• Save cooking water for vegetable stock.

Shredded Beets

"Unbelievably tasty and the quickest way to cook beets. Beware - even beet haters have been known to like these!"

Large beets (scrub, peel if you wish but not necessary, and shred)

- Place a dab of butter in a frying pan. Add shredded beets and sauté, stirring.
- Add a bit of vegetable stock or water.
- Cover and let simmer for 3 to 5 minutes.
- Add a pinch of sea salt, dill or other herbs.
- Leftovers can be added to next day's salad of white cabbage, sprouts or other green leafy bits, along with chopped apple.
- VARIATION: **Auntie Cindy's Baked Beets**: peel beets, chop into bite-size pieces and place in baking dish along with 2 sliced onions, 2 Tbsp (30 mL) beet juice or vegetable stock. Cover. Bake until tender. Sprinkle with crumbles of local goat cheese.

Doughless Pizza GF

"This crust is sooooooo delicious! I used thinly sliced red pepper and some cherry tomatoes from my garden cut in half. Another time I made the crust in a frying pan on the stove! I cooked it on low until it browned, then flipped it over and browned the other side. I ate it like a piece of toast with my meal."

Crust
1 cup (250 mL) cauliflower, riced and cooked
1 cup (250 mL) mozzarella cheese, grated
1 free-range egg, beaten
1 tsp (5 mL) dried oregano
1 tsp (5 mL) garlic salt
1 tsp (5 mL) garlic clove, minced
Pizza sauce
Shredded cheese

Your choice of toppings – need to be pre-cooked since you are only broiling for a few minutes.

"Ricing" The Cauliflower

- Take 1 large head of fresh cauliflower, remove the stems and leaves (into the compost!) and chop the florets into chunks.
- Add to food processor or blender and pulse until it looks like grain. Don't over-do pulse or you will purée it. (If you don't have a food processor or blender, you can grate the whole head with a cheese grater, using less electricity!)
- Place the riced cauliflower into a pot with a tiny bit of water to boil gently for about 12 minutes.
- One large head should produce approximately 3 cups of riced cauliflower. The remainder can be used to make additional pizza crusts immediately, or can be stored in the fridge for up to one week, or added to soup.

Making The Pizza Crust

- Oil a glass pie plate or a cookie sheet (be sure to oil it well).
- In a medium bowl, stir together 1 cup (250 mL) cooked cauliflower, egg and 1 cup of grated cheese.
- Add oregano, minced garlic, and garlic salt. Stir.
- Using your hands, pat the crust mixture into a 9 inch glass pie plate.
- Bake at 450°F (230°C) for 15 minutes. Remove from oven.
- To the crust, add pizza sauce, toppings, and a little shredded cheese.
- Place under a broiler (not too close to the top or it will burn the edges) at high heat just until the cheese is melted, about 3 minutes.

Mushroom and Spinach Fusilli GF (*EASY*) | Serves 4
"This is a working-week-night staple in our house."

1 Tbsp (15 mL) extra virgin olive oil
1 Tbsp (15 mL) butter
2 garlic cloves, minced
1/2 onion, diced

450 g package sliced mushrooms or 1 cup fresh mushrooms,
sliced small
1 chicken or vegetable bouillon cube
3 cups (750 mL) spinach (about 1/2 a bunch chopped)
1 cup (250 mL) plain yogurt, live bacterial culture
Dash of Worcestershire sauce
Pepper to taste
1 package (454 g) fusilli brown rice pasta
Parmesan cheese (optional)

- In a heavy skillet, lightly sauté the garlic and onions in the olive oil and butter until golden.

- Add the mushrooms and bouillon cube and sauté on low heat, covering to retain moisture.

- When mushrooms are brown add the spinach, cover and continue to sauté until the spinach has wilted.

- Turn off the heat. Gently stir in the yogurt and Worcestershire sauce to taste. Do not simmer or the yogurt will curdle. If you want more sauce add more yogurt.

- Add pepper to taste.

- Meanwhile boil the noodles in a large pot of water. Drain and rinse. Toss the hot noodles with the mushroom sauce. Serve sprinkled with Parmesan cheese.

- You can replace spinach with Swiss chard in this recipe. Separate the green leaves from the stalks, chop the chard stalks and sauté with the onions.

Asian Stir-Fry Cabbage with local vegetables
2 Tbsp (30 mL) onion, chopped
1 inch (3 cm) ginger root, minced or grated
1 Tbsp (15 mL) camelina oil or sesame oil
2 Tbsp (30 mL) vegetable stock
1 cup (250 mL) green beans (fresh or frozen), cut in half
1 cup (250 mL) fresh sugar snap peas
1 stalk of celery, diced

3 cups (250 g) red cabbage, shredded
Chopped: kale, dandelion, spinach, Swiss chard or other greens (optional)
1 Tbsp (15 mL) vinegar or lemon juice (to protect the red cabbage colour)
Buckwheat noodles GF
1 tsp (5 mL) sesame seeds

- In a wok or large skillet, sauté onions and ginger in hot oil for one minute.
- Stir in stock. Add beans, peas, celery, and cook for 1 minute, stirring constantly.
- Add cabbage and vinegar or lemon juice, cover and cook over medium heat until cabbage is wilted, about 10 to 15 minutes.
- Serve over buckwheat (soba) noodles. Sprinkle with sesame seeds.

Vegetable Curry with Squash | Serves 6
1 1/2 cups (375 mL) squash, peeled and cubed
1 cup (250 mL) green beans, chopped
1 cup (250 mL) carrots, diced
1 cup cooked chickpeas (optional)
1/2 cup (125 mL) vegetable stock
1 Tbsp (15 mL) extra virgin olive oil
1/2 cup (125 mL) onion, sliced
1 Tbsp (15 mL) ginger root, minced or grated
2 garlic cloves, minced
2 chili peppers (seeded and minced) or a few slices of jalapeno pepper, minced, or chili flakes to taste
1 tsp (5 mL) ground coriander
1 tsp (5 mL) ground cumin
1 tsp (5 mL) ground turmeric
1 tsp (5 mL) garam masala (available in Health Food stores or Indian grocery stores)
1 can diced tomatoes or 2 cups local tomatoes (fresh or frozen),

chopped
1/2 tsp (2 mL) sea salt
1/4 cup (60 mL) fresh coriander or parsley, chopped
1 1/4 cup (310 mL) water

• Serve with local millet or kasha (buckwheat) or brown rice.
• Purchase hot peppers locally and save them in the freezer for use all winter.

Curry Sauce
• In large shallow pot, heat oil over medium heat.
• Sauté onions, stirring frequently until golden, about 10 minutes.
• Add ginger, garlic and chilies and sauté, stirring, until aromatic, about 2 minutes.
• Add coriander, cumin, turmeric and garam masala and sauté, stirring, until aromatic, about 2 minutes.
• Add 1/4 cup (60 mL) water. Bring to a boil, stirring and scraping up brown bits.
• Add tomatoes, sea salt and 1 cup (250 mL) water. Bring to boil, reduce heat and simmer until reduced to about 2 1/2 cups (625 mL), about 15 minutes.
• Stir in coriander or parsley (If you don't have coriander or parsley, toss in some sprouts at the end).
• Add squash, green beans, carrots, and stock; cover and simmer, stirring occasionally, until vegetables are tender, about 12 to 15 minutes.
• Serve with Cucumber Raita. **See Chapter 13: Spreads.**

Adapted from Body Fuel Organics in Regina, SK.

"Don't criticize farmers with your mouth full!"– Sign in a grandfather's barn

Pulses

Lentils, Peas and Beans are gluten-free (GF) and free of Genetically Modified Organisms (GMO).

We can interchange types of lentils, using what we have on hand. Pulses give an affordable bounty of health, support to local farmers, and protection for our food security. DISCOVER!

How to cook pulses? (To cook, **see Chapter 9: Pulses**)

Pulses cook faster if first soaked overnight (except tiny split crimson lentils or small lentils). For QUICK cooking: cover with water, bring to rolling boil, turn off heat and let sit for one hour.

It is a clever strategy to cook a lot and freeze the surplus in 1 or 2 cup batches; flat freezer bags store efficiently. Some folks cook a lot of pulses in a pressure cooker, then preserve in jars.

Much of Saskatchewan's lentil crops go to India and Pakistan, but this happy connection has a dark side. India used to grow all of its own staple food (including lentils) and grew enough to export what was left over. But now, thanks to pressure from the World Trade Organization (WTO), the International Monetary Fund (IMF) and foreign agro-chemical companies, India's farmers have been forced to use their land to grow luxury cash crops like flowers for export to our "first world," and to import food for themselves.

A friend who came to Regina from Pakistan shared recipes featuring our Saskatchewan lentils, Pakistani-style, here adapted slightly, with thanks.

Dal Palak (Lentils and Spinach) | Serves 4
"*Dal*" means "lentil" and "*palak*" means "spinach" in Hindi and Urdu.

1/2 cup (125 mL) small lentils (whatever you have, well washed)
1 onion or local green onion in season, chopped
1 cup (250 mL) vegetable stock or water
2 medium tomatoes (local fresh or home frozen), chopped

1 inch (3 cm) ginger root, minced or grated
2 cups (500 mL) greens: local spinach, kale or dandelion greens,
chopped
2 green chilis, or about 1/2 to 1 Tbsp (7 to 15 mL) chili powder
(to taste - 1 Tbsp is HOT!)
2 Tbsp (30 mL) ground coriander
1/2 tsp (2 mL) garam masala (available in Health Food stores or
Indian grocery stores)

• In a pot, place lentils, onion and water and cook for 10 minutes.

• Add tomatoes, ginger root, greens, chilis and spices.

• Add more water as needed.

• Cook until lentils are soft.

• Serve with millet.

• Leftovers can be stored in small quantities for quick eating.

Beany Burger Mixture | Makes 15 burgers
"Frozen, uncooked, in a bag – these can make a quick meal after a busy day."

1 1/4 cups (310 mL) lentils (any kind)
1/4 cup (60 mL) local quinoa
1/2 cup (125 mL) local millet
3 cups (750 mL) water
1/2 cup (125 mL) quick oats
1 egg, beaten
1 small onion, chopped
3 Tbsp (45 mL) hulled hemp seeds
1 tsp (5 mL) garlic powder
1 Tbsp (15 mL) vegetable bouillon powder
1 tsp (5 mL) black pepper and any other desired seasoning
6 Tbsp (90 mL) salsa, divided
1/3 cup (75 mL) feta cheese, crumbled (optional)
3 Tbsp (45 mL) red pepper, chopped fine (optional)
1/4 cup (60 mL) plain yogurt, (live bacterial culture)

• In a fine sieve, rinse lentils.

- Add to water and cook at low heat at least 30 minutes until soft. Stir occasionally.
- In the fine sieve, rinse quinoa and millet. Add to the lentils for the last 20 minutes of cooking.
- Drain and place in a large bowl.
- Add other ingredients and half the salsa. With hands, work all together thoroughly.
- Form into patties and fry in a little olive oil on medium heat, 3 to 5 minutes per side.
- In a small bowl, mix remaining salsa with yogurt and use as a condiment.
- Serve with vegetables.
- Leftovers (raw or already fried) can be frozen: spread burgers on a cookie sheet lined with wax paper. Leave until frozen stiff, then pack in a bag.

Sauerkraut–Lentil Mash (speedo supper) (*EASY*)
- To sauerkraut, add cooked lentils, fennel or other tasty small seeds or herbs for flavour.
- Serve with sweet potato, and white or purple heirloom potato, mashed together.

Puréed Bean Wrap (speedo supper) (*EASY*)
- Purée cooked beans with a little water or stock.
- Mix beans with flavourings such as ground cumin, curry powder, cayenne pepper, chili powder and herbs.
- Spread puréed beans onto a wrap (corn-free).
- Add chopped vegetables such as tomatoes, celery, peas, local corn, dandelion greens or kale.
- Wrap cosily!

Spicy Lentils and Mushrooms | Serves 4
"Very tasty and easy. Leftovers can be added to soup."

1 Tbsp (15 mL) camelina oil or extra virgin olive oil
1 large onion, sliced
2 garlic cloves, minced
1 inch (3 cm) ginger root, minced or grated
2 cups (500 mL) mushrooms (or less), chopped
3/4 cup (175 mL) brown rice, millet or kasha (buckwheat)
3 cups (750 mL) vegetable stock or water
3/4 cup (175 mL) lentils (any kind except crimson split)
Other garden vegetables such as carrots, kale, cabbage, squash
or parsnip
1 tsp (5 mL) curry powder (or more to taste)
1/2 tsp (2 mL) ground cinnamon
1/4 tsp (1 mL) ground cardamom (optional)
Sea salt and pepper to taste
Fresh local parsley or sprouts, chopped

- In a large pot over medium heat sauté the onion, garlic, ginger and mushrooms until golden 3 to 5 minutes, stirring occasionally.
- Add all other ingredients, except parsley or sprouts.
- Simmer for about 30 minutes.
- Stir in parsley or sprouts. Serve.

Lentil Cheese Loaf | Serves 4
1/2 pound (250 g) cheddar cheese, grated
1 cup (250 mL) cooked lentils
1/2 onion, minced
1/2 cup (125 mL) celery or sweet pepper or mixture, chopped
1/2 tsp (2 mL) sea salt
1/2 tsp (2 mL) ground black pepper
1/2 tsp (2 mL) thyme
1/2 tsp (2 mL) ground cumin (or more spices to taste)
1 garlic clove, minced
1 cup (250 mL) whole grain breadcrumbs, rolled oats or spelt

flakes
1 free-range egg, beaten
1/2 cup (125 mL) milk or hemp beverage

- Mix together cheese, lentils and onions.

- Add egg, bread crumbs, spices, milk or hemp beverage. Mix thoroughly.

- Pour into a greased loaf pan and bake at 350°F (175°C) for 45 minutes.

- Serve with tomato sauce and mashed local potatoes.

North African Stew | Serves 6
"Good nutrition balance, ingredients easy to find and prepare – tastes good."

1 Tbsp (15 mL) camelina oil or extra virgin olive oil
1 large onion, chopped
2 garlic cloves, minced
2 diced medium sweet potatoes (or "yams") or 1 cup butternut squash, peeled and diced
1 cup (250 mL) cooked chickpeas
1/2 cup (125 mL) raw brown rice or local millet (cooks in less time)
2 cups (500 mL) chopped kale or mix with dandelion greens
1 cup (250 mL) carrots, thickly sliced
1 cup (250 mL) zucchini, cubed
1/2 cup (125 mL) raisins
1 tsp (5 mL) ground turmeric
1 1/4 tsp (6 mL) ground cumin
1 1/4 tsp (6 mL) ground ginger
3/4 tsp (3 mL) ground coriander
1/2 tsp (2 mL) ground cinnamon
1/4 tsp (1 mL) ground black pepper
1/2 tsp (2 mL) sea salt
1/2 lemon, juiced
4 cups (1 L) vegetable stock (reserve 1 cup (250 mL) for later)
1/4 to 1/2 cup (60 to 125 mL) of nut butter (optional)

- Mix together nut butter with 1 cup of stock and set aside.
- Add all other ingredients into the slow cooker and cook for 3 hours, or cook on low heat on the stove, stirring occasionally until all vegetables are tender.
- Add nut butter mixture in the last hour of cooking.
- **Variation GF**: serving this over a bed of quinoa, local millet or kasha (buckwheat) would make it gluten-free if you have used gluten-free vegetable stock. Check the fine print, or use your homemade vegetable stock.

Lentil-Millet Pilaf | Serves 4

1/4 cup (60 mL) raisins or dried organic cherries
2 Tbsp (30 mL) leeks or onions, chopped
1 Tbsp (15 mL) camelina oil or extra virgin olive oil
1/2 cup (125 mL) millet
2 tsp (10 mL) pure tomato paste
1 3/4 cups (425 mL) vegetable stock or water
1 or 2 vegetable bouillon cubes
1/4 cup (60 mL) crimson split lentils
1/8 tsp (.5 mL) ground cinnamon
1/4 cup (60 mL) sunflower seeds

- Soak raisins or dried cherries for 10 minutes. Drain and set aside.
- In a large skillet, sauté leeks or onions until golden.
- Stir in the millet and cook for 3 minutes.
- Dissolve tomato paste and bouillon cube in water/stock and stir into the millet.
- Add lentils and cinnamon.
- Bring to a boil, cover, reduce heat and simmer for 20 minutes. Add more water if needed.
- Stir in raisins or cherries and sunflower seeds.
- Pour into oiled 1-quart casserole dish.
- Bake, covered, at 350°F (175°C) for 15 to 20 minutes or until heated through.

Winter Vegetable Stew | Serves 6
"Turnip (or rutabaga) is a prairie vegetable available all winter, hurrah!"

3 Tbsp (45 mL) extra virgin olive oil or sunflower oil

1 large onion, sliced

2 carrots, sliced in rounds

1 parsnip, sliced in rounds

1 small turnip, diced

1/2 large sweet potato (or "yam"), peeled and diced

3 tomatoes (fresh or frozen) or 15 oz can (450 mL)

4 cups (1 L) vegetable stock or water

1 tsp (5 mL) mixed herbs such as dried celery leaves, fresh or dried cilantro, parsley, thyme, basil, dill or oregano (to taste)

1 vegetable bouillon cube or 2 tsp (10 mL) vegetable bouillon powder, or an extra teaspoon of dried herbs (to taste)

1/2 tsp (2 mL) ground black pepper

1 cup (250 mL) cooked chickpeas

Handful of sunflower sprouts or pea shoots or a stalk of celery, sliced thinly

- Sauté vegetables in oil for about 10 minutes. Add liquid as needed.

- Add tomatoes, seasonings and cooked chickpeas with as much vegetable stock or water as needed.

- Simmer until all vegetables are soft but not mushy.

- Serve with leafy green vegetables such as kale or dandelion, Brussels sprouts or broccoli (local fresh or frozen).

Variations:
- Use black beans instead of chickpeas.

- Use any vegetables available (local, organic or chemical free or home frozen): sweet peppers, celery, zucchini, green beans, sprouts, local corn (chopped bite-size) and greens (local spinach, kale, dandelion, Swiss chard, chopped).

- Add fruit such as cherries or cranberries (added near the end).

- Add seasonings such as: ground cumin, curry powder, cayenne or hot sauce.
- Serve with grains to thicken the stew such as: millet, kasha (buckwheat), or wild rice (remember that wild rice needs longer to cook).

Meatless Chili Con Carne | Serves 10

Chana is an East Indian name for chickpeas including garbanzos which we call chickpeas and the brown *Desi* which we call *chana*. These are all grown in Saskatchewan.

2 Tbsp (30 mL) hulled hemp seeds or local quinoa
1 large onion, chopped
2 stalks celery, sliced
3-4 garlic cloves, minced
1 inch (3 cm) ginger root, minced or grated
1 large red sweet pepper, diced
1-2 large fresh or frozen tomatoes, chopped
2 cups (500 mL) canned kidney beans (or home cooked if available)
2 cups (500 mL) canned chickpeas (or home cooked if available)
2 cups (500 mL) canned chana (or home cooked if available)
1 can baked beans in tomato sauce (without pork)
Sea salt and ground black pepper to taste
1 1/2 to 2 Tbsp (22 - 30 mL) chili powder (to taste)

- In a large skillet sauté the onion, garlic, ginger, celery and pepper until golden.
- Add hulled hemp seeds or quinoa and cook for 5 minutes.
- Add remaining ingredients, and then add spices.
- Optional: substitute with pinto or other beans.
- Simmer 20 minutes. If you don't have enough fluid, add tomato sauce, or water.

Hannah's Saskatchewan Stuffed Peppers | Serves 4

Impressive for company! Grand-daughter Hannah is a chef. This is one of her most popular dishes, adjusted for Saskatchewan ingredients. This is quick to put together if you have a quantity of the grains and lentils already cooked, packaged in 1 cup amounts in the freezer. If not, it is a good idea to cook more now, and save the extra for another day.

2 bell peppers (in season)
1 cup (250 mL) pre-cooked wild rice
1 cup (250 mL) pre-cooked local millet
1 cup (250 mL) pre-cooked brown lentils
1 medium onion (diced) or a handful of chives, diced
2 garlic cloves (minced), or 1 tsp (5 mL) garlic powder
Parsley, cilantro or organic celery leaves, minced, or whatever green bits you have

- Pre-cook rice, millet and lentils.
- *To cook wild rice* add 1/3 cup (75 mL) dry rice to 1 cup (250 mL) water, and boil gently for 45 - 60 minutes. Makes 1 cup (250 mL).
- *To cook millet* add 1/3 cup (75 mL) dry millet to 1 cup (250 mL) water, and boil gently for 15 minutes. Makes 1 cup (250 mL).
- *To cook lentils* add 1/2 cup (125 mL) dry lentils to 1 cup (250 mL) water, and boil gently for 25 minutes. Makes 1 cup (250 mL).
- Cut peppers in half lengthwise, clean out seeds.
- Combine all ingredients together. Pack into pepper halves.
- Pour tomato sauce over peppers.
- Cover and bake at 350°F (175°C) for 30 minutes.
- For last few minutes, remove cover and sprinkle with grated cheese.

Harvest Chickpea Vegetable Curry | Serves 8

"Looks gorgeous! Leftovers make good soup next day – just add vegetable stock or water."

2 carrots, sliced
2 cups (500 mL) squash, peeled and cubed
2 cups broccoli florets and tender stems, chopped

1 sweet red pepper, cut in strips

1 small zucchini, cut in chunks

1 red onion, cut in wedges

2 cups (500 mL) cooked chickpeas or 1 can (19 oz / 540 mL) chickpeas, drained and rinsed

1 Tbsp (15 mL) extra virgin olive oil

2 Tbsp (30 mL) ginger root, minced or grated

1 Tbsp (15 mL) curry powder or paste

1 tsp (5 mL) ground cumin

3 garlic cloves, minced

1/4 tsp (1 mL) red pepper flakes, or a dash of hot sauce (to taste)

1/2 cup (125 mL) vegetable stock

1/4 cup (60 mL) chopped fresh coriander or parsley

Serve with local millet, kasha (buckwheat), quinoa or wild rice.

- Cook millet or kasha or quinoa or wild rice. (To cook, **see Chapter 9: Grains**)
- Steam vegetables for 10 minutes until tender crisp.
- Meanwhile in small saucepan, heat oil over medium heat and add ginger and spices, stirring often for 2 minutes.
- Toss with vegetables. Serve over cooked grains.

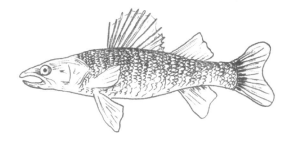

Fish

Use your local or Saskatchewan fish such as whitefish, pike, pickerel, steelhead trout which are available in fish stores. Whitefish is excellent and cheap. Look for Whitefish Fillet Bone-Out because whitefish does have a spine of tiny bones (how can a fish live without a spine?). If it is not de-boned, you can cut out a thin strip of spine and save that to make a fish stock.

Saskatchewan Whitefish in a Pot | Serves 4

2 Tbsp (30 mL) Better Butter
1 medium onion, sliced thin
1 inch (3 cm) ginger root, minced or grated (optional)
3/4 lb (.375 kg) frozen fish, cut into bite-size pieces with scissors
1 tsp (5 mL) ground black pepper (or more to taste)
3 cups (750 mL) cabbage, sliced thin, or mixture of greens such as local spinach, kale, dandelion, Swiss chard, sprouts or wilted lettuce, chopped
1/2 tsp (2 mL) sea salt
2 tsp (10 mL) fresh or dried dill
2 potatoes, peeled and sliced thin
1/2 cup (125 mL) carrots, sliced thin in rounds
1/2 cup (125 mL) milk or hemp beverage
Sprinkle of parsley, sprouts or chives

- Melt butter in a large pot. Add onions and ginger and sauté until golden, for about 3 minutes.
- Add remaining ingredients in layers.
- With lid on, simmer for 30 minutes (or less, only until soft).

Variations:
- Leftovers can become soup chowder the next day.
- Mash leftover Whitefish mixture with chopped onion, milk or hemp beverage, ground black pepper, thyme and garlic powder. Serve with fresh sprouts or chopped parsley with snipped chives on top.

Lake Diefenbaker Steelhead Trout (*EASY*) | Serves 2
"This is my company meal"

1/2 lb (226 g) steelhead fillet
1 inch (3 cm) ginger root, minced or grated
1/2 tsp (2 mL) ground black pepper
1 lemon, sliced thin

- Wash fish (fresh or thawed) and lay in a baking dish.
- Sprinkle on ginger and pepper. Lay lemon slices over top.
- Bake uncovered at 400°F (205°C) for 15 minutes - no more.

Whitefish Nesting in Vegetables | Serves 4
1 Tbsp (15 mL) camelina oil or extra virgin olive oil
1/2 cup (125 mL) onions, chopped, or lots of fresh chives, chopped
1 cup (250 mL) green vegetables such as cabbage, kale, Swiss chard or dandelion greens, chopped
2 cups (500 mL) mixture of other vegetables (whatever you have)
Handful of sprouts (pea, sunflower, lentil, etc.)
Tomatoes, diced
Red sweet peppers, sliced
Mushrooms, sliced,
Carrots, sliced very thin
1 lb whitefish, pike, pickerel or steelhead
1 tsp (5 mL) dried oregano
1 tsp (5 mL) dried basil
1 tsp (5 mL) garlic powder
1/4 tsp (1 mL) ground black pepper
1 Tbsp (15 mL) lemon juice, freshly squeezed (use frozen orange juice if you do not have lemon)
Optional: a few drops of soy sauce or tamari sauce (instead of adding salt), or other spicy sauce

- Sauté the vegetables in oil.
- When vegetables are tender, lay in baking dish, add fish, sprinkle with seasoning, lemon or orange juice and optional sauce.
- Bake for about 10 minutes at 425°F (220°C). Note: If baked too long, even at a low temperature, fish becomes tough.

Spicy Steelhead and Lentils (Dal) | Serves 2

"This recipe is eaten in Pakistan and India, often with Saskatchewan lentils."

2 tsp (10 mL) curry paste or curry powder (mixed in just enough water to make a paste)
14 oz (398 mL) can green lentils, or 1 1/2 cups (375 mL) home cooked
1/4 cup (60 mL) water
2 pieces of Saskatchewan steelhead trout (or other Saskatchewan fish)
Seasoning to taste
3 Tbsp (45 mL) extra virgin olive oil
Juice of 1 lemon
2 large handfuls of baby spinach or other green leaves

- Heat a large shallow pan with a lid over medium heat.
- Add the curry paste and fry briefly, stirring constantly, until sizzling and aromatic.
- Add the lentils with about 1/4 cup (60 mL) water and desired seasoning.
- Heat until simmering, then lay fish on top, skin side up.
- Cover and cook 6-8 minutes until the fish feels firm.
- While fish is simmering mix together the olive oil and lemon juice and season well.
- When fish is cooked, lift it out of the pan and set aside.
- Stir in the spinach and a third of the oil and lemon and cook until the spinach has just wilted.
- Spoon the lentils and spinach onto 2 plates, then set the fish on top.
- Drizzle over the remaining oil and lemon and serve.

Bulanglang – Saskatchewan-Style | Serves 6

Filipino Vegetable Fish Soup, adjusted for Saskatchewan.
Bulanglang is a very popular dish in the Philippines, made from whatever vegetables and spices are available and inexpensive.

Following that principle, we used similar local Saskatchewan vegetables, for a tasty and super healthy soup.

1 Tbsp (15 mL) extra virgin olive oil
1 small onion, chopped
3 garlic cloves, minced
1 inch (3 cm) ginger root, minced or grated
1 medium tomato, sliced
4 cups (1 L) vegetable stock or water
2 Tbsp (30 mL) fish sauce
1 tsp (5 mL) fish sauce (or bagoong isda - fish bagoon)
1/4 squash, cut in cubes; butternut is easy
2 small eggplants, cut in strips, or other local vegetables such as carrots or string beans
1/2 cup (125 mL) green or red peppers, sliced, or 1 bittermelon (ampalaya)
1 cup (250 mL) shredded cabbage, kale (or mulungay leaves)
1 cup (250 mL) spinach, Swiss chard (or alugbati), fresh or frozen
3/4 lb (375 g) Saskatchewan fish such as whitefish, pike or pickerel

- Heat oil in large pot or wok. Sauté onion, garlic, ginger and tomatoes until golden.

- Pour in water, add seasonings and bring to boil.

- Add vegetables and cook gently until vegetables are tender.

- Cut fish in bite-size pieces; if whitefish is not de-boned, cut out the spine. Add fish for the last 10 minutes.

- Serve hot with cooked millet (or steamed rice).

Enjoy your Saskatchewan Bulanglang! With thanks to our Filipino friends.

Meat

Choose animals raised locally, on a small farm, with a caring environment, preferably grass-finished as well as grass-fed. Eat and give thanks to the animals who gave their lives for us.

Mom's Red, Green or Orange Volcanoes or "Stampot" | Serves 8

"Stampot is a Dutch word meaning all cooked together in a pot. For red volcanoes use beets; for green use kale; for orange use carrots."

5-6 medium potatoes, peeled and roughly chopped
3 large beets (or kale or carrots), chopped
1 large onion, minced
1/4 cup (60 mL) butter or yogurt (plain, live bacterial culture) or
2 Tbsp (30 mL) extra virgin olive oil
1/4 cup (60 mL) milk
1/4 tsp (1 mL) sea salt
1/2 tsp (2 mL) ground pepper
1/2 cup (125 mL) fresh parsley, chopped, or other herbs such as dill, thyme or dried celery leaves
1 1/2 lbs (750 g) of smoked or spicy sausage from a local farmer (no nitrites)

- Place the chopped vegetables in a large pot.
- Add a little water, cover, bring to a boil, then reduce heat and simmer until vegetables are tender, about 20 minutes.
- Meanwhile, cook the sausage. Slice and keep warm.
- Make gravy.
- Drain the vegetables well, then mash (but not too smoothly as some lumps are good).
- Mix in the butter, milk and herbs.
- Season with salt and pepper to taste.
- Make a mound of the stampot on the plate and then make a depression in the centre.
- Serve the stampot topped with gravy spilling out of the volcano and with the sliced sausage on the side.

West African Beans with Chicken | Serves 4
"Versions of this recipe are made throughout West Africa and everywhere else in the world where West Africans live."

1 cup black-eyed beans
1 chicken breast
4 medium tomatoes
1 medium onion
1/2 green pepper
1 garlic clove
1 chicken bouillon cube (optional)
Sprinkling of black pepper
2 Tbsp (30 mL) olive oil

- Wash beans, soak for about 6 hours, strain and pour off liquid.
- Cut chicken into chunks, add black pepper, and cook in olive oil.
- Blend tomatoes, onion, green pepper and garlic.
- Add the beans, blended vegetables and bouillon cubes to the chicken, simmer about 20 minutes.
- Serve over rice.

Moroccan-style Chicken | Serves 4
Choose chicken that is local, organic or raised naturally.

1 Tbsp (15 mL) extra virgin olive oil
4 chicken thighs (remove some skin)
1 large garlic clove, minced or 1 tsp (5 mL) garlic powder
1 tsp (5 mL) ground cumin
1 tsp (5 mL) ground coriander
1 tsp (5 mL) paprika
1 medium onion, diced
1/4 cup (60 mL) local red lentils
7 oz (200 mL) can whole tomatoes, chopped or 1 cup local fresh or home frozen
1 Tbsp (15 mL) ketchup
1 cup (250 mL) vegetable or chicken stock
1 cinnamon stick

1/2 cup (125 mL) local dried cherries, or dried apricots, chopped
Mint leaves (fresh, for garnish)

- In an ovenproof casserole dish place the onions, lentils, tomatoes, ketchup, vegetable stock and dried fruit. Lay chicken thighs on top.
- In a small bowl, mix the garlic, cumin, coriander and paprika together. Spread the spice mixture all over the chicken.
- Bake at 350°F (175°C) about 1 1/2 hours (or less).
- Toward the end, cover loosely with aluminum foil.
- Serve with local millet, kasha (buckwheat), wild rice, or imported brown rice.

Wild Meat Marinade

2 Tbsp (30 mL) ketchup
1/4 tsp (1 mL) onion salt
Ground black pepper to taste
Garlic powder or garlic cloves (to taste), minced

- Combine ingredients, pour over chosen meat, seal the container and refrigerate for 24 hours.
- Every several hours, turn the meat over so every part benefits.

Lamb Stretchy Stew | Serves 6

Use just a taste of lamb, from a local farmer only. Stretch good meat by adding lentils and lots of vegetables.

1/2 lb (226 g) ground lamb, frozen (more for a larger family or for 2 meals)
3/4 cup brown or green lentils
Lots of vegetables such as potatoes, onion, garlic, carrots, parsley, turnip, squash, cabbage and Brussels sprouts, coarsely chopped
Leafy greens such as kale, dandelion and Swiss chard, chopped
Any herbs you have, especially mint leaves, oregano and dill

Ground black pepper to taste

A few drops of tamari sauce

If the lamb is still frozen (because you forgot to take it out of the freezer), put it in a medium-hot frying pan, scrape often and stir until it is thawed and somewhat browned.

- Wash lentils in sieve under running water.
- Add lentils and vegetables (except greens) to meat pan.
- Add vegetable stock or water as needed.
- Cover, simmer until all are soft.
- Stir in herbs and sauce.
- Add chopped greens just to wilt (no more than 5 minutes).
- Store leftovers in jars. This can be frozen for another night's quick supper.

Bison Meatloaf with Glaze | Serves 6

1 lb (454 g) bison (ground)

1 cup (250 mL) whole grain breadcrumbs or local rolled oats

1 or 2 free-range eggs, beaten

1/2 medium onion, diced

1 garlic clove, minced or 1 tsp (5 mL) garlic salt

1 carrot, shredded

1/4 cup (60 mL) 2% milk or hemp beverage

1 sprig of fresh rosemary (leaves removed from stem)

1/4 tsp (1 mL) sea salt
1/2 tsp (2 mL) ground black pepper

• Mix the above ingredients and pack into a greased casserole dish. Cover with glaze.

Glaze
1/4 cup (60 mL) local honey
3 Tbsp (45 mL) vinegar
1/2 cup (125 mL) saskatoon berries or dried cherries
1 Tbsp (15 mL) soy sauce or tamari sauce
1/4 cup (60 mL) boiling water

• Mix glaze and spread over meatloaf.
• Bake at 350°F (175°C) for 1 hour.

Venison and Wild Rice Stew | Serves 8

3 1/2 lbs (1.6 kg) shoulder of venison, cut into 1 inch cubes
6 to 9 cups (1.5 to 2 L) water (add water as needed)
2 yellow onions, chopped
1 1/2 cups (375 mL) wild rice, washed in cold water
4 cups of water
Local herbs of your choice
2 tsp (10 mL) sea salt (to taste)
1/4 tsp (2 mL) ground black pepper

• Lightly brown the venison cubes.

• Place the meat, water and onions in a large heavy pot and simmer uncovered for 3 hours or until venison is tender.

• Meanwhile, mix together wild rice, herbs, salt and pepper. Add water, cover and simmer this mixture for 20 minutes.

• Add rice mixture to meat, stir together and simmer uncovered for about 20 minutes more or until rice is tender and most of the liquid is absorbed.

Treat Bites: Baking and Desserts

Baking

To "grease" pans or muffin tins, you need only a tiny drip of vegetable oil in a dish and a little square of wax paper, or a clean finger to rub the oil across the pan. Bread loaves need more, and cookies are better without "greasing." There is no need to pay money or use up more of Earth's resources with paper liners, or even packaged spray.

It is important to eat a variety of grains, not just wheat.

If using honey, reduce oven temperature slightly.

To freshen a biscuit or bannock another day, swipe under the cold water tap, wrap in aluminum foil, warm in oven 350°F (175°C) for about 10 minutes.

Cheese Biscuits (*EASY*) | Makes 20
"A favourite with soup or for between-meal nibbling."

2 cups (500 mL) kamut wheat flour
Variation: 1 1/2 cup (375 mL) wheat flour, 1/2 cup (125 mL) chickpea flour
GF variation: 3/4 cup (175 mL) quinoa flour, 3/4 cup (175 mL) buckwheat flour, 1/2 cup (125 mL) sweet rice flour
3 tsp (15 mL) baking powder
1/2 tsp (2 mL) sea salt
1/4 cup (60 mL) Better Butter
1 cup (250 mL) old cheddar cheese, grated
1 cup (250 mL) milk or hemp beverage

- In a large bowl, mix dry ingredients together. Cut in butter.
- Add cheese and milk and mix just enough.
- Drop onto lightly greased sheet by spoonfuls. Shape with fingers (flatten if you like).
- Bake at 400°F (205°C) for 15 minutes.

Adapted from the *More-With-Less Cookbook* by Doris Janzen Longacre.

Flax Bread | Makes 1 loaf
1 1/2 tsp (7 mL) active dry yeast
1 1/2 cups (375 mL) warm water
3 Tbsp (45 mL) local honey
1 Tbsp (15 mL) camelina oil or sunflower oil
1/2 tsp (2 mL) sea salt
1 cup (250 mL) ground flax seed
1 1/4 cups (310 mL) whole wheat flour (whole grain is best)
1 3/4 cups (425 mL) unbleached bread flour or unbleached white flour

- In a large bowl, dissolve the yeast in 2 Tbsp (30 mL) of the water. Set aside until bubbly, about 5 minutes.
- Mix in the honey, oil, salt and the remaining 1 1/4 cups (310 mL) water.
- Add the ground flax seed, whole wheat flour and 1 cup (250 mL) of the bread flour. Mix well.
- Stir in enough of the remaining bread flour to make a soft, kneadable dough.
- Turn the dough out onto a lightly floured surface.
- Knead for 10 minutes, or until smooth and elastic.
- Grease a 9 x 5 inch loaf pan with oil. Shape the dough into a loaf and place in the pan.
- Cover and let rise in a warm place until doubled in size (about 1 hour).
- Bake at 350°F (175°C) for 40 to 45 minutes, or until the loaf is browned on top and sounds hollow when tapped. Cool.

Country Seed Bread for breadmaker (*EASY*) | Makes 1 1/2 lb loaf
1 1/8 cups (280 mL) warm water
3 Tbsp (45 mL) camelina oil or extra virgin olive oil
2 Tbsp (30 mL) local honey
3 cups (750 mL) whole grain wheat flour (kamut works well)
1 tsp (5 mL) sea salt

2 Tbsp (30 mL) sesame seeds

1 Tbsp (15 mL) poppy seeds

2 Tbsp (30 mL) hulled hemp seeds

2 Tbsp (30 mL) hulled raw sunflower seeds

1 or 2 Tbsp (15 mL or 30 mL) ground flax seeds

3 tsp (15 mL) gluten flour

2 tsp (10 mL) active dry yeast

• Set bread maker control for whole wheat, and light colour.

Adapted from *Healthy Breads with the Breadmaker* by Silke Alles and Sieglinde Janzen, Alive Books.

Breakfast Health Muffins | Makes 12 muffins
"Just delicious!"

1/2 cup (125 mL) Fair Trade sugar or part local honey

1/2 cup (125 mL) unsweetened home-made apple sauce

1/4 cup (60 mL) water

3/4 cup (175 mL) camelina oil or extra virgin olive oil or sunflower oil

1 cup (250 mL) buttermilk or sour milk (2% milk with 1 Tbsp (15 mL) vinegar to curdle)

1 free-range egg

2 Tbsp (30 mL) molasses

1/2 cup (125 mL) wheat germ or hulled hemp seeds

1/4 cup (60 mL) sesame seeds

1/4 cup (60 mL) ground flax seed

1 tsp (5 mL) baking soda

1 1/2 tsp (7 mL) baking powder

1/2 tsp (2 mL) sea salt

1 cup (250 mL) natural bran, rolled oats or chickpea flour
(Avoid processed bran cereals because they can be loaded with sugar and additives.)

1 tsp (5 mL) ground cinnamon

1 tsp (5 mL) ground ginger

2 cups (500 mL) whole grain flour such as kamut or spelt
3/4 cup (175 mL) dried cherries, raisins or a mixture of both

- Soak dried cherries for 10 minutes. Drain.
- Blend together sugar or honey; apple sauce or sprouts, oil, milk, egg and molasses.
- In a large bowl, stir together all dry ingredients.
- Add wet mixture to dry ingredients and stir together just to moisten.
- Add fruit and stir gently.
- Lightly oil muffin tin and nearly fill each cup.
- Bake at 375℉ (190℃) for 15 minutes or until top springs back. Do not overcook – they burn easily.

Berry Lentil Muffins GF | Makes 18 muffins
1 1/2 cup (375 mL) cooked small lentils
1 cup (250 mL) buckwheat flour
1/2 cup (125 mL) quinoa flour
1/2 cup (125 mL) sweet rice flour
1 Tbsp (15 mL) baking powder
1/2 tsp (2 mL) sea salt
1/2 tsp (2 mL) ground cinnamon
1/2 tsp (2 mL) ground allspice
1/2 tsp (2 mL) ground ginger
1/2 cup (125 mL) camelina oil or sunflower oil
1/2 cup (125 mL) local honey
1/2 cup (125 mL) orange or apple juice
2 free-range eggs
1 1/2 cups (375 mL) raspberries, cherries, saskatoon berries, blueberries, haskaps, or cranberries

- In a large bowl combine all dry ingredients: flour, baking powder and seasonings.
- In a blender combine oil, honey, juice, eggs and 1 cup (250 mL) of the lentils.

- Purée until smooth. Add to dry mixture.
- Gently stir in fruit and the rest of the lentils.
- Bake at 375°F (190°C) for 20 minutes.
- Non-GF variation: use 2 cups of wheat flour.

Adapted from *The Big Book of Little Lentils*, Saskatchewan Pulse Growers.

Broccoli Muffins (*EASY*) | Makes 12 muffins
"A surprising treat with soup."

2 cups (500 mL) kamut, spelt or quinoa flour (or mixture)
1/2 cup (125 mL) chickpea, rye or buckwheat flour (if using chickpea flour, mash it smooth with a fork)
1 1/2 tsp (7 mL) baking powder
1 tsp (5 mL) baking soda
1/2 tsp (2 mL) sea salt
1 1/2 cups (375 mL) frozen broccoli florets or fresh broccoli with stems, diced
1 Tbsp (15 mL) extra virgin olive oil
2 Tbsp (30 mL) Better Butter
1 large free-range egg
1/2 cup (125 mL) milk or hemp beverage
1 cup (250 mL) vegetable stock or water
4 tsp (20 mL) fresh basil (chopped) or 2 tsp (10 mL) dried basil
1 tsp (5 mL) dried dill crumbled
1/2 cup (125 mL) hard cheese, grated

- In a large bowl, stir all the dry ingredients together except cheese.
- Blend the wet ingredients and herbs (not the broccoli) together briefly, then add broccoli to blender.
- Whiz for 2 seconds; check that broccoli bits don't get too mashed.
- Add wet mixture to dry and stir together just to moisten.
- Drop into oiled muffin tins.
- For the last 5 minutes, sprinkle grated cheese on top of each muffin.

• Bake at 375°F (190°C) for 15 to 18 minutes.

Inspired by the Green Spot organic restaurant in Regina, SK.

Pumpkin Buckwheat Muffins GF | Makes 20 muffins

1 cup (250 mL) buckwheat flour
3/4 cup (175 mL) quinoa flour
3/4 cup (175 mL) kamut flour (GF variation: use sweet rice flour instead of kamut)
1/2 cup (125 mL) hulled hemp seeds
1 tsp (5 mL) baking soda
1 1/2 tsp (7 mL) baking powder
1/2 tsp (2 mL) sea salt
2 tsp (10 mL) ground cinnamon
1/2 tsp (2 mL) ground ginger
1/2 tsp (2 mL) ground nutmeg
1/4 cup (60 mL) Fair Trade sugar
1/2 cup (125 mL) camelina or extra virgin olive oil or sunflower oil
3 free-range eggs
1/2 cup (125 mL) local honey
2 1/2 cups (625 mL) cooked pumpkin or squash (mashed)
1/2 cup (125 mL) walnuts, chopped or sunflower seeds
1/2 cup (125 mL) organic dried cherries or raisins

• Soak dried cherries for 10 minutes. Drain and set aside.

• In large bowl, mix dry ingredients.

• Blend wet ingredients in a blender: oil, eggs, honey and pumpkin until pumpkin is smooth.

• Add wet mixture to dry ingredients and stir together just to moisten.

• Add nuts and fruit and stir gently.

• Lightly oil muffin tin and nearly fill each cup.

• Bake at 350°F (175°C) for about 15 minutes.

Cherry Spice Muffins GF | Makes 12 muffins

Buttermilk, when used in muffins, reduces the need for oil.
Buttermilk is high in calcium & protein, low in calories and makes
super good muffins.

1 cup (250 mL) quinoa flour
1/2 cup (125 mL) chickpea flour
3/4 cup (175 mL) sweet rice flour
1/4 cup (60 mL) Fair Trade sugar
1 1/2 tsp (7 mL) baking powder
1 tsp (5 mL) baking soda
1 tsp (5 mL) ground cinnamon
1/4 tsp (1 mL) ground allspice
1/2 tsp (2 mL) ground cloves
1/4 tsp (1 mL) sea salt
2 Tbsp (30 mL) hulled hemp seeds
3/4 cup (175 mL) dried cherries or other dried fruit
1 1/4 cup (310 mL) buttermilk
1/4 cup (60 mL) water or 1/4 cup (60 mL) soaking water from the
fruit
1/4 cup (60 mL) apple or orange juice concentrate
1/4 cup (60 mL) camelina oil or sunflower oil
1 free-range egg

• Soak dried fruit for 10 minutes. Drain and set aside. Save the
  soaking water.
• In large bowl, mix dry ingredients together.
• Mix wet ingredients in a blender or bowl: buttermilk, juice
  concentrate, oil and egg plus 1/4 cup (60 mL) of water or fruit
  soaking water.
• Add wet mixture to dry ingredients and stir together just to
  moisten.
• Add fruit and stir gently.
• Lightly oil muffin tin and nearly fill each cup.
• Bake at 375°F (190°C) for 18 to 20 minutes.

Whole Grain Bannock (*EASY*) | Makes 20 pieces

Bannock, or Le Galet, was brought from Scotland to Canada by the Scottish fur traders. They, with their First Nations wives, passed it down to their modern descendants. Bannock has remained essential to First Nations and Métis culture.

2 cups (500 mL) whole grain flour (kamut, spelt or wheat)
1 cup (250 mL) unbleached white flour
Variation: this also works well with 3 cups of whole grain flour and no white flour.
1 tsp (5 mL) sea salt
2 Tbsp (30 mL) baking powder
1/4 cup (60 mL) camelina oil, sunflower oil or 1/4 cup (60 mL) butter, melted
1 1/4 cup (310 mL) water
Optional: 1/2 cup saskatoon berries, other berries or raisins; 1Tbsp (15 mL) caraway seeds or 1 tsp (5 mL) cinnamon

- Mix all ingredients together, adding the fruit and other extra ingredients last.
- Spread on a floured counter and pat flat to desired thickness.
- Cut out shapes with a knife, or drop from a spoon onto an oiled baking sheet and press to shape with hands.
- Enjoy with local fruit jam or "spread" (has less sugar).

Desserts

Yogurt Delight (*EASY*)
"My 3 minute company dessert."

Yogurt (plain, live bacterial culture): 1/2 cup (125 mL) per person
Fruit such as: raspberries, cherries, saskatoon berries, blueberries, haskaps, cranberries, chopped or stewed apples or stewed rhubarb
Real maple syrup, local organic fruit topping or liquid local honey
Home-made granola, muesli or hulled hemp seeds
A taste of grated ginger root (optional)

- Mix fruit and sweetener into the yogurt.

- Top each with muesli or granola, and garnish with a cherry.
- Serve in pretty bowls or glass goblets.

Cottage Cheese Kuchen | Serves 12
"Kuchen was a favourite of my German ancestors."

Base
1 cup (250 mL) flour
Pinch of sea salt
1 tsp (5 mL) baking powder
2 Tbsp (30 mL) Fair Trade sugar
1/2 cup (125 mL) butter
1 free-range egg beaten
1 Tbsp (15 mL) milk

- Combine first four ingredients, blend in butter until crumbly.
- Add egg and milk.
- Mix and press into a 9 x 12 inch pan.

Filling
2 cups (500 mL) cottage cheese
3/4 cup (175 mL) Fair Trade sugar
1 cup (250 mL) unsweetened applesauce
1 tsp (5 mL) vanilla
2 Tbsp (30 mL) tapioca or arrowroot starch
A sprinkle of cinnamon

- In a blender, combine filling ingredients. Blend & pour over base. Sprinkle with cinnamon.
- Bake at 350°F (175°C) for 45 minutes or until set.

Cherry Lentil Brownies | Makes 18 pieces

3 free-range eggs
1/2 cup (125 mL) Better Butter
1/2 cup (125 mL) dark lentils, cooked
1/2 cup (125 mL) Fair Trade cocoa
1 cup (250 mL) Fair Trade sugar
1/2 tsp (2 mL) sea salt
1 tsp (5 mL) vanilla
3/4 cup (175 mL) frozen organic cherries
1 cup (250 mL) chickpea flour
1/3 cup (75 mL) Fair Trade chocolate chips

- In a blender whiz together eggs, butter, lentils, cocoa, sugar and salt until the lentils are a paste.
- Add cherries and whiz very briefly to make sure that cherries don't get too mashed.
- In a bowl, add flour then add wet ingredients to flour and stir until blended together.
- Add chocolate chips and stir.
- Spread in well-greased 13 x 9 inch (or smaller) cake pan.
- Bake at 350°F (175°C) for 22 minutes or until toothpick or knitting needle inserted in the centre comes out clean.
- Serve with slices of fresh fruit.

Adapted from *The Big Book of Little Lentils*, Saskatchewan Pulse Growers.

Chocolate-Chickpea Brownies GF (*EASY*) | Makes 12 pieces
"A very tasty treat, super quick and easy to make."

1 cup (250 mL) Fair Trade chocolate chips
2 cups (500 mL) home-cooked chickpeas or a 19 oz (540 mL) can chickpeas, rinsed and drained
4 free-range eggs
1/4 cup (60 mL) Fair Trade sugar
1 tsp (5 mL) baking powder

1/2 tsp (2 mL) baking soda
1/2 cup (125 mL) walnuts, chopped or dried organic cherries

• Soak dried cherries for 10 minutes. Drain. Drink the soaking water for a treat!

• Melt the chocolate on very low heat, stir often until smooth.

• In blender or food processor combine the chickpeas, eggs, sugar, baking powder and baking soda. Whiz until completely liquefied. Add melted chocolate and blend until smooth, stopping to scrape down the sides and make sure the chocolate is well mixed in.

• With a spoon, gently stir in the nuts, or cherries.

• Oil a 9 x 9 inch cake pan, dust with cocoa and spread batter in pan.

• Bake at 350°F (175°C) for 30 minutes or until toothpick or knitting needle inserted in the centre comes out clean.

• Cool in pan before cutting into squares.

Cocoa Beet Cookies GF | Makes 24
"You wouldn't know without being told!"

1 3/4 cups (425 mL) rolled oats
GF variation: quinoa flakes
1/2 cup (125 mL) Fair Trade cocoa
3 cups (750 mL) whole wheat, spelt or kamut flour
GF variation: 2 cups buckwheat or quinoa flour, 1 cup sweet rice flour
1/2 tsp (2 mL) sea salt
2 tsp (10 mL) baking powder
1 tsp (5 mL) baking soda
3/4 cup (175 mL) Better Butter or margarine
1 cup (250 mL) Fair Trade sugar
3 free-range eggs
1 tsp (5 mL) vanilla
1 cup (250 mL) cooked beets, chopped (may be frozen)
1 1/2 cups (375 mL) beet juice, water, milk or hemp beverage
1 cup (250 mL) saskatoon berries, dried organic cherries or

raisins (or mixture)
Optional: 1/2 cup (125 mL) walnuts, washed and chopped or lentil sprouts, chopped – nutty local lentil sprouts give a chewy texture.

- Soak dried cherries or dried raisins for 10 minutes. Drain. In a large bowl, mix dry ingredients.
- In blender, whiz all wet ingredients including beets, until well blended. Add to dry ingredients.
- Optional: add fruit, walnuts or lentil sprouts.
- Drop by spoonfuls onto a cookie sheet.
- Bake at 350°F (175°C) for about 15 minutes.

Rhubarb Torte GF | Makes 9 pieces

"On the prairies rhubarb is one of the first fruits of the season (although actually it is a vegetable). Rhubarb is a good source of vitamin C. In the early years, oranges were not available, so rhubarb gave major health benefits. Women used the stalks in many ways in jam and in baking. This recipe was passed down from my great-grandmother in Manitoba."

Crust

3/4 cup (175 mL) quinoa or buckwheat flour
1/4 cup (60 mL) sweet rice flour
1/8 tsp (.5 mL) sea salt
1/2 cup (125 mL) softened butter

- Mix all together then press into a 9 x 9 inch pan.
- Bake at 325°F (160°C) for 20 minutes.

Filling

2 Tbsp (30 mL) quinoa or buckwheat flour
1/3 cup (75 mL) cream, whole milk or 2% milk
1 cup (250 mL) Fair Trade sugar
3 free-range egg yolks
2 1/4 cups (560 mL) rhubarb (fresh or frozen, chopped)

- In a saucepan, combine flour and cream and mix until smooth.

- In a small bowl, beat egg yolks (leave whites aside).
- Add the remaining filling ingredients and cook on low to medium heat, stirring often until thick and tender, about 20 minutes. Pour over baked crust.

Topping
3 free-range egg whites
1/2 tsp (2 mL) cream of tartar
2 Tbsp (30 mL) Fair Trade sugar

- Beat egg whites until peaks form. Add cream of tartar and sugar and beat a bit more.
- Pour topping over rhubarb filling.
- Bake at 400°F (205°C) until the meringue is browned, about 2 minutes only. Watch, as it browns quickly.

"Looked and tasted impressive for New Year's Eve; with last summer's frozen rhubarb, a promise of spring."

Melting Moments Cookies (*EASY*) | Makes 24 small, fancy cookies
"This is an old recipe adapted from Grace Gunn of East River St. Mary's, Pictou County, N.S. In Saskatchewan these are called Birds' Nests."

1/2 cup (125 mL) Fair Trade or brown sugar
1/3 cup (75 mL) butter or Better Butter
1 free-range egg
1 tsp (5 mL) vanilla
1 1/2 cups (375 mL) whole grain flour such as wheat, kamut or spelt
3/4 tsp (175 mL) baking soda
1 Tbsp (15 mL) hulled hemp seeds
Local fruit jam or spread

- In small bowl, beat egg. Mix with butter, sugar and vanilla or whiz all in a blender.
- In a larger bowl, mix flour, baking soda and hulled hemp seeds.
- Stir in wet ingredients, except jam.
- Roll into small balls, place on ungreased pan, not touching.

- Poke a hole in each ball and fill with jam.
- Bake at 350°F (175°C) for about 15 minutes.

Eatmore Bars (*EASY*) | Makes 12
"Very good, and easy."

1/2 cup (125 mL) peanut butter (pure, ground in a Health Food store)
1/2 cup (125 mL) local honey
1 cup (250 mL) carob chips or Fair Trade chocolate chips
1 tsp (5 mL) vanilla
1 1/2 cups (375 mL) large flake rolled oats
2 Tbsp (30 mL) hulled hemp seeds
1 cup (250 mL) mixture: organic raw almonds (unsalted, toasted, and chopped), ground flax seeds, organic coconut or whatever you have.

- Bring peanut butter and honey to a boil.
- Add carob or chocolate chips, vanilla and remaining ingredients.
- Press into a greased flat pan.
- When cool, cut into bars. These can be stored in the freezer.

Nanna's Gingerbread (*EASY*)

"Molasses has nothing to do with Saskatchewan. But we who are now at home here, come with our memories of our first foods and the love that went with them. When I was a child in Halifax during the war (around 1942) my mother would send me with a glass jar to a shop near the harbour where a large keg had a spigot. When I turned the tap, out poured molasses, straight from the West Indies. There was always molasses on the table, even if there was no butter. A molasses sandwich was a staple. During the war, eggs were rationed so my mother got extra cracked eggs from a farmer. This recipe has been adjusted for modern health."

3/4 cup (175 mL) molasses
3/4 cup (175 mL) butter
2 free-range eggs
1 cup (125 mL) boiling water
2 tsp (10 mL) baking soda
2 3/4 cups (675 mL) flour (whole grain wheat, spelt, kamut or quinoa) minus 1 Tbsp (15 mL) flour
2 Tbsp (30 mL) ground ginger
3 tsp (15 mL) ground cinnamon
1/2 tsp (2 mL) sea salt
1/2 cup (125 mL) saskatoon berries or blueberries (fresh or frozen)

- Blend or mix the eggs, butter and molasses by hand.
- Add boiling water to baking soda in a measuring cup - look out - it bubbles up!
- In another bowl, mix together the flour, ginger, cinnamon and salt.
- Pour wet ingredients into dry ingredients and mix well, adding the saskatoon berries.
- Bake in a well-oiled 9 x 9 inch pan at 350°F (175°C) for 25 to 30 minutes.
- Serve topped with hot applesauce, made from gleaned Saskatchewan apples stewed with small bits of plain ginger root.

Chapter 14:
Kids Cook and Eat

"Vegetables are crucial for child mental and physical development and for disease prevention." – Danielle Nierenberg

How to get them to eat the good food?

Make mealtime a happy time. Start with preparing the food. Begin with setting the table. Sit and eat together as a family. By making a rule of no technology devices at the dinner table, you can make eye contact with each other and actively listen. Share the "goodies" and the "nasties" of each one's day. Ask open-ended questions: "What was your favourite part of school today? What was one activity you did in gym class – or art class - today? What beautiful or surprising or funny thing did you see today?" Talk about the food you are eating. By questioning where each food item came from, how it got to the grocery store or Farmers' Market and which people helped get it from farm-to-fork, you make others more aware of what they are putting in their mouths and how it got there. Thank the Earth for the food on the table and thank the cook/parent/child who helped prepare the meal or set the table.

Have the one-bite of everything rule. It does work, after many tries. Don't make them finish something they don't like – just makes them hate it (and you) more.

Serve small portions. They can come back for seconds or thirds.

Make surprises. When my children came to their grandparents for dinner, Nanna served the meal of good food onto their plates. Then in turn, they passed their plates up to Grampy. He creatively turned each plate into a scene – a "pretty dinner." It worked like a charm!

Another family has a surprise supper with unusual utensils, or no utensils at all! Try eating soup with a fork, or dinner with a giant serving spoon! What fun!

Cut fruit into interesting shapes. Combine something liked with something new or less-liked such as a peanut butter on sliced apple sandwich, or one white slice with one whole grain slice – working up to all whole grain.

Engage them in food preparation. Using healthy stuff, create new combinations, new goofy food names and food pictures. They can cut up veggies or fruit, with safety scissors if they are too young for a knife.

Kristine Beer, Alex's mom wrote: "*I make sure every meal/snack has something fresh: cut up fruit on the side, fresh cut up cucumber, or cherry tomatoes. Alex gets a fresh fruit and veggie EVERY DAY in his lunch. If he doesn't want breakfast, a smoothie does it, with an organic banana, strawberries, 1 Tbsp hulled hemp seed, 1/2 tsp chia seeds and rice milk.*"

Alex, age 5, wanted to help with this book, so he wrote his own recipe for quesadillas.

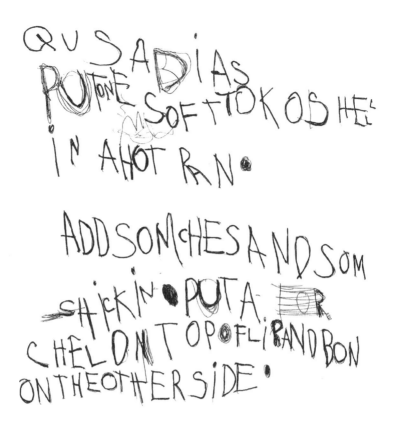

Quesadillas

Put one soft taco shell in a hot pan.
Add some cheese and some chicken.
Put a shell on top.
Flip and brown on the other side.

The "Litterless" Lunch

Many schools across Canada are encouraging parents to pack a "litterless lunch" for their child. This eco-friendly initiative causes all family members to be environmentally aware of the waste that is produced daily through pre-packaged lunch-kits with "one-time use" lunch items such as plastic spoons, plastic wrap and juice boxes, etc.

Here are some green tips to help empty the landfills and save Earth's resources:

Pack stainless steel or other reusable utensils instead of disposable plastic ones.

Pack a safe reusable drink container instead of a disposable juice box or pouch, can, or plastic bottle.

Pack lunch items in reusable containers or bags. When possible, avoid using plastic wraps, plastic bags, and aluminum foil; probably healthiest are cloth, waxed paper or paper towel (which is recyclable).

Pack a cloth napkin instead of a paper napkin.

Avoid purchasing small, pre-packaged items. Buy food in larger containers and then divide it up at home.

Pack complete lunch in a lunch box or cloth draw-string bag instead of relying on throw-away paper or plastic bags. They could make and decorate their own cloth lunch bags.

Baby Food

Baby food should be only organic, because babies are extremely susceptible to pesticides.

Cook the food, with no sugar or salt. You can combine vegetables and fruits especially for your child.

Blend to the texture suitable for your child's age.

Put in an ice-cube tray, freeze, then put in plastic bags, labeled.

Thaw a cube when needed.

To thaw: put in a non-plastic dish, set in hot water. Never put baby food in a microwave because it destroys the nutrients.

Be sure to test the temperature before serving to the baby.

Children are known to love plain, unsweetened yogurt, if they start young enough.

Perfect Baby Food

Bake butternut squash with lots of fresh butter on it. Mash it up. Spoon it into eagerly awaiting baby mouths.Yummmm.

Easy, Fun Cooking

Also **see Chapter 13: Snacks and recipes marked *EASY*.**

Egg in a Hole | For each person
1 slice whole grain bread (try grains other than wheat: such as spelt, rye)
1 egg, free-range
1 tsp (5 mL) Better Butter or softened butter
1 tsp (5 mL) olive oil

- Butter both sides of the bread.
- Cut a hole in the centre of the bread. Set the bread aside. You could cook the hole piece too.
- Crack the egg into a small bowl, remove any shell bits. Check for freshness.
- Place the buttered bread in the pan.
- Pour the egg slowly and carefully into the hole.
- On medium heat, cook the egg about 2 minutes until the clear part turns white.
- With the egg flipper, turn the bread/egg over.
- Cook about 2 minutes more.
- Flip onto a plate. Dress up with some vegetables, like a slice of local tomato, cucumber or sprouts.
- You could shake a tiny bit of grated cheese onto the egg.

Pizza Buns | For each child
1 whole grain bun or English muffin
1 Tbsp (15 mL) or more, tomato sauce or other sauce
1/4 cup (60 mL) cheddar cheese, grated
1/4 cup (60 mL) or more, vegetables, chopped
Optional: 1/4 cup (60 mL) cooked chicken, chopped

- Cut bun or muffin in half.
- Spread sauce on each half.
- Put vegetables and optional chicken on top.
- Cover with grated cheese.
- Place on a baking sheet.
- Place in oven. Bake for 5 – 10 minutes at 350°F (175°C) until pizza is golden brown and edges are crispy.

Fruit Parfait | For each child
Fresh fruit, local if possible: saskatoons, cherries, raspberries, strawberries or organic banana. Cut in small chunks if necessary
Granola
Plain yogurt, probiotic live culture

- Build layers: yogurt, granola, yogurt, topped with fruit.
- Drizzle with a little maple syrup or liquid honey.

These three recipes were adapted with thanks to the *After School Cooking Club* at REACH, www.reachinregina.ca.

Chapter 15:
Stories

"Just" Eating
by Laura Sundberg

"In September 2012, our church organized a potluck supper to promote Every Bite, and test the recipes within. We were challenged to use local ingredients in whatever we brought. I don't have much time to cook, so I decided that a trip to the local Farmers' Market was my best option.

It was a beautiful day – blue sky and a hint of fall crispness in the air. I strolled along the Market Plaza viewing the many local products for sale. There were varieties of handiwork, honey and beeswax candles, meat and baking, fruit and vegetables, and much more. I was delighted and overwhelmed with the many food options to choose from. For the potluck challenge, would I bring a locally grown and baked cherry pie? Would I buy vegetables and make soup?

As I walked around I had a visit with a church member whose son and daughter-in-law own "Over the Hill Orchards." I had a brief chat with a local Rabbi, who was also out shopping. I learned about different coloured carrots from a local grower. Finally I decided on a dozen cobs of corn for the potluck supper, and a sweet treat from "Over the Hill" for my family.

Buying locally does take more effort, but it has its rewards. Buying locally can give us connections with the farmers, the Earth, and our community. I call it "Just Eating" – a spiritual journey of mindfulness. Sacred energy comes to us from sun, rain and Earth. Sacred energy mixes with the energy of farmers and all who pick, or bake, or contribute to the food that we consume – to nurture all of us. With every bite let us eat justly, and be nurtured into action – caring for the Earth and the common good."

Laura Sundberg is minister and friend of Creation, at St. James United Church in Regina, Saskatchewan.

Journey to Health
by Kristine Beer

"When my son was born 6 years ago, I noticed that there was a lot of baby food on the market, but I didn't like some of the ingredients – hydrogenated oil and salt being the biggest culprits. So I decided to make my own baby food. Since then, both my son and I have next to no wheat and no dairy in our diet. I also have developed a soy allergy, and have found that there is soy in everything from salad dressing to margarine, and in almost every prepared food, boxed and frozen. I even found soy in some brands of tea! Then I learned that practically all soy is genetically modified. So off to the Internet I went in search of recipes. I started making my own tomato sauce and broth, breads and muffins. I started a garden and we eat fresh veggies and herbs from it all summer long. For what I don't grow, we get the majority from the Farmers' Market or from local gardens. We also made the switch to get our beef from a local farmer. When my son and I get a cold, it is with much less frequency and severity, and we have not needed antibiotics in over 2 years! I believe that our changes have made us healthier people, both inside and out."

Kristine Beer is a lively musician / teacher who radiates joy and beauty, and inspires creativity in young and "not-so-young."

Growing for Grace
by Jordan Fieseler

"It all started when I walked into Eat Healthy Foods and was offered a Pink Lady apple. It was the best apple I'd ever tasted – and – it was organic. Almost a decade has passed since that first bite. My wife, Laura, and I have learned much about the importance of locally grown and chemical-free food growing. Now we produce a lot of our own food. With 6 community garden plots, a neighbour's backyard and some out-of-town space, we grow most of the vegetables we consume in a year, along with some beans and grains. With so much production, we have had to develop many preservation techniques: pressure and water-bath canning, lacto-fermenting, dehydration, and cold storage.

One of the best things about growing and "putting up food" (food preserving) is the sheer creativity of these endeavours. There are so many different vegetables to grow, designs for gardens, recipes to try to create and meals to share. We must talk with other people to learn their techniques, their secrets and insights. We eat, we contemplate, and we talk. Then we realize we have enriched our communities – we feel safe, we feel more content. We see other people inspired to action by our self-sufficient endeavours. We see folk who weren't gardening and preserving, suddenly jumping into it – tearing up their lawns, growing beautiful food. They tell that when life gets really stressful, they can go into the garden, pull some weeds, and be re-centred. I think that is what many people are missing: having quiet time with the Earth, where both are being nurtured and fulfilled.

When we connect with one another to grow and share food, we are nourishing ourselves and others, in body, mind and spirit. We are caring for the Earth. A most satisfying co-operative experience of ours is taking care of two shared hives of bees on a friend's land. There is nothing like sweating hard using a hand-crank to extract honey in a 35°C garage while sharing a bottle of home-brewed mead; then sitting down to a table overflowing with food tended by the hands that have come together for grace."

Jordan Fieseler works with Nature to create Sacred Earth Soaps, and grow fabulous organic food for family and friends.

Guerilla Gardener
by Sr. Elaine Weisgerber

"Houses across from my former apartment building were leveled, and developers were nowhere to be seen. For this aging nun, here was an opportunity! I borrowed a shovel from my brother, did a walk-about, and decided on a piece of land only 6 feet square. In no time, lettuce, spinach, carrots and zucchini were happily growing and providing my daily salad.

During the entire summer I was greeted by passersby. They wondered what I would do if the developers moved in or if my garden were attacked by thieves or vandals. No one warned me about the real garden raiders – rabbits! When I caught one feeding on the lettuce, I gathered twigs and spread them between the rows. No more rabbits!

When I was labeled a "guerilla gardener" I thought people were referring to the muscle I needed to prepare the plot! It is great learning this new terminology, and even more wonderful to gather fresh food, every day, from the Earth."

Sr. Elaine is always ready to welcome new experiences with grace and zest, even aging.

Musqua and the Greedy Ones
by Eleanor Brass

"The summer was very dry and growth was slow, so there were only a few berry patches and the berries themselves were small. In seasons such as these, it was customary for a camp to go together to pick all the berries they could, so that everyone would have an equal chance to get some food for the family.

But there were always some greedy and grasping individuals who only thought of themselves. Early one morning a couple left the village before sunrise, planning to quietly come back with their berries while everyone was still sleeping. They thought that no one would ever know.

They took along their birch bark baskets and were picking at the berry patch when suddenly they heard a loud crash of breaking brush, indicating that something was approaching them.

"Musqua! Musqua! A bear! A bear!" cried the man. They became so frightened that they dropped their container, berries and all. The bear was close on their heels by this time, growling and snorting fiercely. They were so terrified that they ran as fast as they could, finally reaching the camp. The noise had aroused everyone and the people just stood outside their teepees and looked at them. The couple were so humiliated and ashamed that they disappeared into their teepee and didn't show themselves for several days.

After this, every time anyone tried to get ahead of the others in picking berries they were sure they could hear the growls and grunts of the bears, reminding them that they must think of the others."

The saskatoons picked by our grandmothers and great-grandmothers by the sackful were dried in the sun. Laying skins on the ground in the morning, when the sun was beginning to get hot, they spread the berries out and left them there all day. When the sun sank in the sky, they gathered them up before the dew came.

From the book *Medicine Boy: and Other Cree Tales*, 1979. Reprinted with permission from the Glenbow Museum, Calgary, Alberta.

> **Mrs. Eleanor Brass**, born on Peepeekeesis Reserve in southern Saskatchewan, devoted much of her life to spreading under-standing about her Cree people and their traditions. She worked as an information officer for the Saskatchewan Department of Agriculture; and later at Peace River Friendship Centre as pup-peteer, story teller and writer.

Chapter 16:
Glossary:
Nutrients and Food Sharing

Nutrients

Acidophilus is a friendly bacteria that assists in the digestion of proteins, has anti-fungal properties, helps reduce cholesterol and enhances the absorption of nutrients. The flora in a healthy colon should consist of 85% acidophilus. Usually available in milk yogurt or coconut yogurt.

Antibiotics are pharmaceutical drugs developed to kill bacteria causing infections in the body or stop these bacteria from reproducing. These infections threaten the immune system's ability to function. Antibiotics have been effective in saving lives. But the over-use of antibiotics is now leading to the bacteria developing "super bugs" resistant to antibiotics. Factory farmed animals receive high doses of antibiotics. This can put people who eat factory farmed animals at higher risk.

Antioxidants are natural compounds in foods that neutralize free radicals and help protect and detoxify the body. They can be obtained from food sources such as green leafy plants, sprouted grains, fresh fruit (such as berries and cherries) and vegetables (eggplants are highly effective) whole grains, pulses and nuts. Bright colours – orange, red, blue, purple and green – are a clue that antioxidants are present in that food. Some herbs (garlic) also have antioxidant properties.

Carotene is an antioxidant which can be changed by the body into vitamin A.

Essential Fatty Acids (EFAs) are just that – essential to every living cell in the body for rebuilding and producing new cells. Our body needs to be supplied with these from food sources since the body cannot make them. Omega-3 EFA gets a lot of attention, because it interrelates with a host of body functions: heart health, brain and nervous system function, and eye health; its lack is correlated to depression. Rich amounts of Omega-3 are found in deep water fish (whether in ocean or fresh water, fish get Omega-3 from leafy green algae growing on the bottom). Other good sources of Omega-3 are fish oils, flaxseed oil, hemp seeds, chia seeds, pumpkin seeds, walnuts, green leafy plants, and animals who eat green leaves and grasses. For health, recent studies confirm that we need an equal balance of Omega-3 and Omega-6. But North Americans typically eat 20 times more Omega-6 than Omega-3. Highest sources of Omega-6 are grain-fed meat (not grass-fed) and cheap, mass-pro-duced oils such as corn oil and soybean oil. Eating a lot of processed food puts the eaters at risk because the food industry is a heavy user of corn and soybean oil.

Heat destroys EFAs and creates free radicals. Most corn, soy and canola oils have been processed, refined and heated. EFA foods and oils are best added to cooked foods after the foods have finished cooking.

Flavonoids: are powerful antioxidants found naturally in plants. They give antibiotic and anti inflammatory benefits – just another reason to eat our fruit and vegetables!

Free Radicals are atoms or groups of unpaired atoms that can damage cells. This damage weakens the immune system, so the body becomes vulnerable to developing infections and various degenerative diseases such as heart disease and cancer. Free radicals may be formed in various ways such as exposure to radiation (microwaves), toxic chemicals and cooking with fats in high temperatures as in fried foods and charcoal foods.

Gluten is a protein found in all wheat but more in modern wheat, less in oats, barley, rye, ancient wheat (spelt and kamut). Some people are gluten sensitive or intolerant and eating these grains, particularly the modern wheat varieties, can cause moderate to severe intestinal damage and possibly difficulty in absorbing nutrients. Note that heritage Red Fife wheat has its long history in Saskatchewan and has been preserved in its original form, unmodified. Red Fife flour is always grown organically and is stone-ground, thus preserving the germ. Although Red Fife seems to have high gluten content, still it is well tolerated by many who are sensitive to other wheats.

High Glycemic foods and beverages contain lots of easily digested carbohydrates that can quickly raise blood sugar levels, giving a burst of energy, then a flop. By suddenly increasing the amount of actual sugar (glucose) that goes into the blood, high glycemic foods cause wild fluctuations in blood sugar level. The more that carbohydrate-containing foods are processed or overcooked, the higher their glycemic level becomes. Keeping whole foods in their natural, unprocessed state is a key factor in retaining a food's lower glycemic level. Some of the most common high glycemic foods we eat are white flour foods, cane or corn sugars (high fructose corn syrup), white rice, processed or overcooked potatoes.

Low Glycemic foods are digested more slowly, raising blood sugar in a regulated and gradual way. Because of this they stay in your digestive tract longer, giving better control of appetite and delaying hunger. Balanced blood sugar decreases the risk of developing insulin resistance. From years of science-based nutritional studies it is now accepted that eating lower glycemic foods is associated with decreased risk of many serious diseases and health problems. Eating whole, natural foods, lots of vegetables, fruits, pulses, some lesser amounts of whole grains and grass-fed meats and poultry can give the advantage of maintaining stable energy and enjoying a healthier body.

Phytochemicals act as antioxidants and include many of the beneficial substances in our food. "Phyto" means "plant" in Greek. Most plants produce natural chemicals in order to defend themselves from pests and diseases. These protecting benefits are then passed on to the plants' eaters. Organically grown plants produce more phytochemicals in order to increase their natural ability to protect themselves because no synthetic chemicals do it for them. Thus many organic plants turn out to have increased antioxidant, anti-inflammatory benefits for humans, especially tough and edible wild plants like dandelions, lamb's quarters, purslane and chickweed.

Probiotics are beneficial bacteria found in the digestive tract and vital for proper digestion. They help prevent the overgrowth of pathogens. These beneficial bacteria are found in foods such as buttermilk, cheese, kefir, miso, sauerkraut, tempeh, umeboshi and "probiotic" or "live culture" yogurt. Regularly eating these foods helps keep the digestive system operating effectively.

Protein are chains of amino acids linked together providing the structure for all living things. Amino acids that are not needed by the body are processed by the liver and kidneys. An over-abundance of unneeded amino acids can stress these organs. In our culture we tend to eat more proteins from meat than our body needs, putting a strain on the kidneys and liver. These organs also have to deal with the many toxins our bodies take in, especially from factory-farmed meat as well as medications. Eating too much meat has also been implicated in increasing obesity.

Good sources of protein besides meat, poultry, fish, milk, and cheese are eggs, pulses (beans, peas, lentils and chickpeas), nuts, seeds and grains. Having a balance of amino acids, hulled hemp and quinoa are among the most complete of plant proteins.

Trans-fatty acids are created by an industrial process that adds hydrogen to an unsaturated fatty acid, resulting in processed vegetable oils. As these vegetable oils are solidified and stabilized through the hydrogenated process they don't go rancid as quickly as normal so are valued for their long shelf life.

Trans-fats cause many major health problems. They increase the total cholesterol level and LDL levels in the blood while reducing the good HDL levels. They harm the cardiovascular system and interfere with the body's use of Omega-3. The Heart and Stroke Foundation of Canada states that trans-fats are 5 times more harmful than saturated fats.

Foods still containing trans-fats are margarine, baked goods, cookies, donuts, cakes, chips, crackers, most fried foods, and French fries. Any product that has "partially hydrogenated vegetable oils" or "vegetable oil shortening" contains trans-fats. Trans-fat levels in Canada remain higher than recommended by the World Health Organization. High consumption of trans-fats is responsible for thousands of cardiac deaths in Canada.

Food Sharing

Community Supported Agriculture (CSA) helps consumers get closer to the farmers and connect with our food. Unlike Farmers' Markets, where consumers buy a few days' worth of fruit and vegetables, Community Supported Agriculture allows consumers to purchase a small share of the crop. Participants pay up front for a full season's share. You receive an exciting variety of fresh-picked vegetables regularly throughout the growing season, delivered to a convenient pick-up location. You also share the farmer's risk, whatever the weather. On the farmer's website you can check out where your food is coming from, and in some cases you can visit the farm and even help with the work. Some CSA farms also offer meat and eggs, and preserved foods through the winter.

Fair Trade logo guarantees that the foods grown by small farmers in the developing world have gained a minimum fair price for the producers, decent working conditions plus an investment in their communities. Fair Trade encourages organic methods of agriculture, preserves ecosystems, protects human rights and trade unions, and bans child labour. The fair trade movement is based on democratic organization, and aims to transform society's values. This indepen-dent international certification is based on yearly inspections. Fair Trade Canada is our independent, national, non-profit Fair Trade certification organization.

Monoculture can be hundreds of acres planted with one crop, usually drenched with synthetic fertilizers and pesticides. Massive machinery replaces the work of many people. Monoculture depletes the soil, leaves no wild food for essential bees or beneficial insects, birds and butterflies.

Permaculture is widely recognized as the most adaptive and durable framework for transforming culture and agriculture in the post-industrial world. Permaculture creates sustainable communities of plants, animals, soils, water, energy, buildings and human needs in permanent health-giving relationships. Permaculture is designed to regenerate, reflecting patterns in Nature. Permaculture seeks to build interconnections allowing for energy efficiency and abundance of yield. Permaculture has the capacity to produce food with fewer resources, leave natural habitats alone, restore soils, assist certain kinds of wildlife where allowed, and address factors creating climate change. Most importantly, its positive approach attracts and inspires people to take action.

Slow Food Movement. Slow Food is about taking time to savour "good, clean, fair" food in a community of eaters. People in Slow Food groups cherish food produced locally in harmony with Earth's processes (such as grass-finished animals, chemical-free fruit and vegetables), and shun processed convenience food. Slow Food is about families and friends eating mindfully together instead of on the run. It's about really appreciating Earth's gifts of food.

Sustainable Agriculture cares for long-term economic vitality, which depends on caring for soil, water, air, workers and animals. Sustainable agriculture cares for the interworking of all elements that could go on supporting food into the indefinite future.

> *"In India, ecological and organic agriculture is referred to as 'ahimsic krishi' or 'non-violent agriculture' because it is based on compassion for all species."*
> – Vandana Shiva

The Western Diet is a new phenomenon in the world's history. In the early 20th century, medical professionals in Africa such as Dr. Albert Schweitzer were amazed at the absence of diseases common today, until the arrival of Western food, particularly refined flour and sugar and processed "store food." In 1939, Canadian-born Weston Price published his widespread research of the health degeneration among Indigenous Peoples. Although their various traditional diets were very different, the common denominator of good health, he concluded, was to eat a traditional diet consisting of fresh foods from animals and plants grown on soils that were themselves rich in nutrition.

> *"Commercial synthetic chemical fertilizers increasingly destroy the health-giving qualities of the soil."*
> – Michael Pollan

Chapter 17:
Vision Voices

"Everyone has the right to a standard of living adequate for the health and well-being of himself and his family, including food."

   – Universal Declaration of Human Rights, Article 25

"Why do you spend your money on that which is not food? Listen carefully to me, and eat what is good, and delight yourselves in life-giving food."

   – Isaiah 55:2

"War destroys life. It also destroys food systems for the living."

   – Cathleen Hockman-Wert in *Simply in Season*

"The fields of the poor might yield much food, but it is swept away by injustice."

   – Proverbs 13:23

"I believe in a gospel that reaches right into the digestive system."

– Menno Wiebe: with the Mennonite Central Committee he started more than 100 Native Gardening Projects on First Nations Reserves

"My view of the planet was a touch of divinity."

– Edgar Mitchell (the sixth man on the moon)

"Addressing the ecological crisis requires a new level of consciousness, where we understand that we belong to the larger family of life on Earth."

– Wangari Maathai. *Replenishing the Earth*

"Every meal we ingest is solar sacrifice."

– Bruce Sanguin, *Darwin, Divinity, and the Dance of the Cosmos: An Ecological Christianity*

"Every day, the world produces twice the amount of food needed to nourish everyone. Yet, every day, one billion people are hungry; most of them are farmers."

– Saskatchewan Council for International Cooperation Global Action Calendar 2013

"Every aspect of our lives is, in a sense, a vote for the kind of world we want to live in."

– Frances Moore Lappé

"How can we live within the limits the planet gives us? If we keep raiding Earth's fridge this way, there will be nothing left to eat."

– Salli McFague, *A New Climate for Theology: God, the World, and Global Warming*

Resources on the Culture and Politics of Food

Books

Clarke, Tony. *Inside the Bottle: An Exposé of the Bottle Water Industry*. Ottawa: CCPA, 2005.

Costa, Temra. *Farmer Jane: Women Changing the Way We Eat.* Layton, Utah: Gibbs Smith, 2010.

Davis, William. *Wheat Belly: Lose the Wheat, Lose the Weight, and Find Your Path Back to Health.* Toronto: HarperCollins, 2011/2012.

Desmarais, Annette Aurélie. *La Via Campesina: Globalization and the Power of Peasants.* Black Point, NS and Winnipeg: Fernwood Publishing, 2007.

Eaton, Emily. *Growing Resistance: Canadian Farmers and the Politics of Genetically Modified Wheat*. Winnipeg: University of Manitoba Press, 2013.

Elton, Sarah. *Locavore: From Farmers' Fields to Rooftop Gardens: How Canadians are Changing the Way We Eat.* Toronto: HarperCollins, 2010.

Gibbons, Gail. *The Honey Makers*. New York: HarperCollins, 2000. An educational, lovingly illustrated book looking at the wonders of a honey bee's life.

Gustafson, Katherine. *Change Comes to Dinner: How Vertical Farmers, Urban Growers, and Other Innovators are Revolutionizing How America Eats.* New York: St. Martin's Griffin, 2012.

Herriot, Trevor. *Grass, Sky, Song: Promise and Peril in the World of Grassland Birds.* Toronto: HarperCollins, 2009.

Hicks, J. Morris. *Healthy Eating, Healthy World: Unleashing the Power of Plant-Based Nutrition.* Dallas: Benbella Books, 2011.

Holtslander, Cathy, Darrin Qualman, Alexander Irvin and Rick Sawa. *Beyond Factory Farming: Corporate Hog Barns and the Threat to Public Health, the Environment, and Rural Communities.* Saskatoon, SK: Canadian Centre for Policy Alternatives-Saskatchewan, 2003.

Kallas, John. *Edible Wild Plants: Wild Foods from Dirt to Plate.* Layton, Utah: Gibbs Smith, 2010.

Kingsolver, Barbara. *Animal, Vegetable, Miracle: A Year of Food Life.* Toronto: HarperCollins, 2007.

Ladner, Peter. *The Urban Food Revolution: Changing the Way We Feed Cities.* Gabriola Island, BC: New Society Publishers, 2011.

Lappé, Frances Moore. *Hope's Edge: The Next Diet for a Small Planet.* Cambridge, MA: The Small Planet Institute, 2003.

Maathai, Wangari. *Replenishing the Earth: Spiritual Values for Healing Ourselves and the World.* New York: Doubleday, 2010.

McFague, Sallie. *A New Climate for Theology: God, the World, and Global Warming.* Minneapolis: Fortress Press, 2008.

Miller, Sally. *Edible Action: Food Activism and Alternative Economics.* Black Point, NS and Winnipeg: Fernwood Publishing, 2008.

Moss, Michael. *Salt Sugar Fat: How the Food Giants Tricked Us*. Toronto: McClelland & Stewart, 2013.

Pollan, Michael. *Omnivore's Dilemma: a Natural History of Four Meals.* New York: Penguin, 2007.

—— *In Defense of Food: An Eater's Manifesto.* New York: Penguin, 2008. Also available as an audiobook on five CDs.

Rodale, Maria. *Organic Manifesto: How Organic Farming Can Heal Our Planet, Feed the World, and Keep Us Safe.* New York: Rodale, 2010.

Sanguin, Bruce. *Darwin, Divinity and the Dance of the Cosmos: An Ecological Christianity.* Kelowna, B.C.: Wood Lake Publishing, 2007.

Savage, Candace. *Bees: Nature's Little Wonders. Madeira Park, B.C.: Greystone Books, 2008.*

Shiva, Vandana.

—— *Biopiracy: The Plunder of Nature and Knowledge.* Brooklyn, NY: South End Press, 1999.

—— *Soil Not Oil: Environmental Justice in an Age of Climate Crisis*. Brooklyn, NY: South End Press, 2008.

—— *Stolen Harvest: The Hijacking of the Global Food Supply.* Cambridge, MA: South End Press, 2000.

—— *Water Wars: Privatization, Pollution and Profit.* Cambridge, MA: South End Press, 2002.

Smith, Alisa and J.B. MacKinnon. *100-Mile Diet: A Year of Local Eating.* New York: Random House Canada, 2007.

Weatherford, Jack. *Indian Givers: How Native Americans Transformed the World.* New York: Ballantine, 1988/2010.

Wesley, Andrew. *The Ecologist Guide to Food: Lifting the Lid on What We Put in our Mouths.* London, UK: Leaping Hare Press, 2014. Includes information about animal suffering, human rights abuses, destruction of ecosystems, pollution and waste.

Whittman, Hannah, Annette Aurelie Desmarais and Nettie Wiebe (eds). *Food Sovereignty: Reconnecting Food, Nature and Community*. Black Point, NS and Winnipeg: Fernwood Publishing, 2010.

──*Food Sovereignty in Canada: Creating Just and Sustainable Food Systems*. Black Point, NS and Winnipeg: Fernwood Publishing, 2011.

Worldwatch Institute. *2011 State of the World: Innovations that Nourish the Planet*. Washington, DC, 2011.

Cookbooks

Alles, Silke and Sieglinde Janzen. *Healthy Breads with the Breadmaker: Delicious and Nutritious Bread Creations. Vancouver, BC: Alive Books, 2000.*

Appelhof, Mary. *Worms Eat My Garbage: How to Set Up and Maintain a Worm Composting System.* Flower Press, 1997 2nd ed. Clear, fun illustrations for grade 5 level to adult.

Beach, Mark and Julie Kauffman. *Simply in Season Children's Cookbook*. Scottdale, PA: Herald Press, 2006. Stunning, fun photography by Jenna Stoltzfus.

Canadian Lentils. *The Big Book of Little Lentils.* Saskatoon, SK: Saskatchewan Pulse Growers, 2012. www.lentils@saskpulse.com or 306-668-9988.

Dales, Phyllis and Bruce Dales. *Cranberry: The Cure for Common and Chronic Conditions.* Vancouver, BC: Alive Books, 2000.

Day, Sonia. *Incredible Edibles: 43 Fun Things to Grow in the City*. Richmond Hill, ON: Firefly Books, 2010.

Ehman, Amy Jo. *Prairie Feast: A Writer's Journey Home for Dinner.* Regina, SK: Coteau Books, 2010.

Finkelstein, Paul. *26 Super Foods: with Disease-Fighting Recipes.* Toronto: Reader's Digest Association (Canada), Fall 2011.

Gail, Peter. *Dandelion Celebration: A Guide to Unexpected Cuisine*. Cleveland, OH: Goosefoot Acres, 1990/1994.

Katz C. J. *Taste: Seasonal Dishes from a Prairie Table*. University of Regina: Canadian Plains Research Centre Press, 2012. Stunning to look at, this award-winning book focuses on Saskatchewan food and farmers.

Lind, Mary Beth and Catherine Hockman-Wert. *Simply in Season: Recipes that Celebrate Fresh, Local Foods in the Spirit of More-With-Less.* Scottdale, PA and Waterloo, ON: Herald Press, 2009. Commissioned by the Mennonite Central Committee to promote understanding of how the food choices we make affect our lives and the lives of those who produce the food. This attractive book can be a supplement to *Every Bite Affects the World.*

Mars, Brigitte. *Dandelion Medicine: Remedies and Recipes to Detoxify, Nourish, Stimulate.* Pownal, VT: Storey Books, 1999.

Meyer, Mary Clemens and Susanna Meyer. *Saving the Seasons: How to Can, Freeze, or Dry Almost Anything.* Scottdale, PA.: Herald Press, 2010.

Films

Addicted to Plastic. Dir. Ian Connacher. 2008. Canada. 85 min. Reveals the history and worldwide scope of plastics pollution, investigates its toxicity and explores solutions.

Bacon, the Film. Dir. Hugo Latulippe. 2002. Canada, 52 min. Exposes hog farms in Quebec.

Bitter Seeds. Dir. Micha X. Heled. 2011. USA. 88 min. Multi-award winning film about the farmer suicide epidemic in India and the link to GM seeds.

Dirt! The Movie. Dir. Rosow and Benenson. 2009. USA. 86 min. Shows inside the wonders of the soil beneath our feet. One of its awards: "*Best film for our future.*"

El Contrato. Dir. Min Sook Lee. 2003. Canada: 51 min. Shows the unjust conditions of Mexican workers on several tomato farms in Leamington, Ontario.

Food Inc. Dir. Robert Kenner. 2008. USA. 94 min. Exposes corporate farming in the U.S.; guaranteed to change our eating habits.

Fresh the Movie. Dir. ana Sofia joanes. 2009. USA. 72 min. Celebrates people who are re-inventing our broken food system, with Michael Pollan, Will Allan and Joel Salatin.

Genetic Roulette: The Gamble of our Lives. Dir. Jeffrey M. Smith. 2012. USA. 60 min. Exposes the documented health risks of genetically engineered foods.

Hijacked Future: Who Controls the Seed Controls our Food. Dir. David Springbett. Canada. 43 min. 2008. Shows how the chain of food production from seed to plate is in the hands of fewer and fewer companies.

Last Call at the Oasis. Dir. Jessica Yu. 2012. USA. 105 min. Shows why the global water crisis will dominate this century.

Mad Cow Sacred Cow. Dir. Anand Ramayya. 2009. Canada, 53 min. Indian-Canadian film-maker tells a universal story connecting the beef crisis, the farm crisis, and the global food crisis. Illustrated in Saskatchewan and India; narrated by Nettie Wiebe and Vandana Shiva.

The Meatrix. Dir. Louis Fox. 2006. USA. 4 min. In this animated short film, Leo the Pig learns the truth about factory farms, and how consumers can make a change to support small family farms.

More than Honey. Dir. Markus Imhoof. 2012. Germany. 95 min. An in-depth look at honeybee colonies in California, Switzerland, China, and Australia.

Queen of the Sun: What Are the Bees Telling Us? Dir. Taggart Siegel. 2010. USA. 82 min. Beekeepers, scientists and philosophers include Michael Pollan, Gunther Hauk and Vandana Shiva. Must watch!

Seed: the Untold Story. Dir. Taggart Siegel. 2014. USA. This is the David and Goliath battle against the high-tech industrial seed companies to preserve seed biodiversity and food security.

Silence of the Bees. Dir. Doug Shultz. 2007. USA, 53 min. PBS Nature.

The Story of Bottled Water. Dir. Annie Leonard. 2010. USA. With lively animation, Annie Leonard creates compelling education in a few minutes.

The Story of Food. USC. 2009. Canada. Short animated film about our broken food system and what we can do about it.

To Make a Farm. Dir. Steve Suderman. 2011. Canada, 74 min. Five young people without farming experience embark on making their farming dreams a reality. Their story is told with exquisite beauty and hope.

Urban Roots. Dir. Mark Macinnis. 2011. USA: Tree Media. Inspiring documentary about spontaneous urban farming in devastated Detroit.

Water on the Table. Dir. Liz Marshall. 2010. Canada. 49 min. "*A moral look at the survival of the species*" featuring Maude Barlow.

Websites

Aluminum:
www.theguardian.com/environment/2010/jun/13/mining-aluminium-tribes-india-jagger. "*First hand observation of the impact of aluminum mining in India.*" Search for: environmental damage from Bauxite mining in Jamaica.

Bananas:
Banana Link: www.bananalink.org.uk. "*Working toward a fair and sustainable banana and pineapple trade.*"
Foro Emaus: members.tripod.com/foro_emaus/2ing.html
Euroban in Solidarity with Foro Emaus

BC Food Systems Network:
www.fooddemocracy.org

Bees:
Sierra Club Canada: www.sierraclub.ca

Butterflies:
World Wildlife Fund: www.wwf.org. Search for: World Wildlife Fund butterflies

Chocolate:
www.facts-about-chocolate.com/fair-trade-chocolate

Climate Change:
Oxfam Canada:
www.oxfam.ca/our-work/publications/growing-disruption-climate-change
Pembina Institute: www.pembina.org
Sierra Club Canada: www.sierraclub.ca

David Suzuki Foundation:
www.davidsuzuki.org/what-you-can-do

Fish:
www.davidsuzuki.org/issues/oceans

www.Seachoice.org

Food Security: Canada
CHEP (Child Hunger and Education Program), Saskatoon:
    www.chep.org or 306-655-4575
REACH (Regina Education and Action on Child Hunger):
    www.reachinregina.ca or 306-347-3224
Food Secure Canada: www.foodsecurecanada.org
Food Secure Saskatchewan:
    www.foodsecuresaskatchewan.ca. A coalition of individuals and groups
    working toward achieving just and dignified access to food for all citizens
    which is safe, nutritious, culturally appropriate and local.

Food Security: Global
Canadian Foodgrains Bank: www.foodgrainsbank.ca/videos.aspx
ETC Group: www.etcgroup.org

Food Sovereignty:
La Via Campesina: Videos at www.youtube.com/user/videosviacampesina and
    Vimeo.com/viacampesina.

United Church of Canada: *Toward Food Sovereignty for All*. Search for: United
    Church Toward Food Sovereignty for All.
Unitarian Service Committee (USC): www.usc-canada.org/food-crisis; Canadian
    Seed Security and Seeds; Biodiversity, Women Farmers: www.seedsecurity.
    ca/en

Food Tank:
www.foodtank.com

Fruit:
Canadian Gardening Magazine: www.canadiangardening.com
Fruit for Thought (Regina): fruit-for-thought-regina.blogspot.com
Out of Your Tree (Saskatoon): www.outofyourtree.org
Over the Hill Orchards (certified organic): www.overthehillorchards.ca
Saskatchewan Fruit Growers' Association: www.saskfruit.com

Genetically Modified Organisms:
Bill Moyers: BillMoyers.com. www.billmoyers.com/segment/
    vandana-shiva-on-the-problem-with-genetically-modified-seeds
Canadian Biotechnology Action Network (CBAN): www.cban.ca
The Institute for Responsible Technology: www.responsibletechnology.org
Non-GMO Project: www.nongmoproject.org
Non-GMO Shopping Guide: www.nongmoshoppingguide.com
Quaker Institute: www.quakerinstitute.org. *Genetically Modified Crops: Promises,
    Perils, and the Need for Public Policy*, Quaker Institute for the Future, 2011.

Habitat:
Canadian Wildlife Federation: www.wwf.org
Rainforest Action Network: www.ran.org
Sierra Club Canada: www.sierraclub.ca

National Farmers' Union:
National office in Saskatoon: www.nfu.ca or 306-652-9465

Organic Organizations:
Beyond Pesticides (USA): www.beyondpesticides.org. "*Protecting health and the environment with Science, Policy and Action*"
Canadian Biotechnology Action Network: www.cban.ca
Canadian Organic consumer info site in French and in English:
        www.OrganicBiologique.ca
Organic Consumers' Association: www.organicconsumers.org
Saskatchewan Organic Directorate (SOD): www.saskorganic.com
Saskatchewan Organic Marketing and Processor Directory:
        www.agriculture.gov.sk.ca/organic_directory

Pesticides:
Farmworker Justice: www.farmworkerjustice.org/content/pesticide-safety
Northwest Center for Alternatives to Pesticides: www.pesticide.org
Pesticide Action Network: www.panna.org/issues/frontline-communities/
        farmworkers

Permaculture:
www.permaculturenews.org
www.permaregina.ca
www.permasask.ca
www.prairiepermaculture.com
www.vergepermaculture.ca

Plastics:
www.eartheasy.com
www.en.wikipedia.org/wiki/Plastic#Production_of_plastics. Outlines the toxins
        produced and the environmental and energy costs.
www.greenlivingonline.com
www.lifewithoutplastic.com/en/about-plastic/why-is-plastic-a-problem
www.sheknows.com/food-and-recipes/articles/945847/
        hidden-dangers-of-food-storage-containers

Pulses:
Alberta Pulse Growers: www.pulse.ab.ca
Manitoba Pulse Growers: www.manitobapulse.ca
Pulse Canada: www.pulsecanada.com/food-health/recipes

Saskatchewan Pulse Growers: www.saskpulse.com

Saskatchewan Eco Network:
www.econet.ca

Saskatchewan Environmental Society:
www.environmentalsociety.ca

Sustainable Living:
www.eartheasy.com
www.greenlivingonline.com

Shrimp:
Mangrove Action Project: www.mangroveactionproject.org
www.globalissues.org/news/2011/09/13/11156
www.greenpeace.org/international/en/campaigns/oceans/aquaculture/
    shrimp-farming
www.nrdc.org/living/shoppingwise/meals-mass-destruction-shrimp.asp
www.seafoodsource.com/en/global-aquaculture-issues/23934-

Slow Food:
www.slowfood.com

Water:
The Council of Canadians: www.canadians.org/water
Natural Resources Defense Council (USA): www.nrdc.org/water

Worldwatch Institute:
www.worldwatch.org

Index

Thanks and Acknowledgements

Thanks go first to Treaty Four land on which this book sprouted and grew. We are all Treaty people. We are honoured that Dr. Nettie Wiebe has written the Foreword.

Every Bite Affects the World has grown out of the caring and contributions of a host of people.

Thanks to the many who shared their recipes, submitting them to the creative process which often adjusted or combined them. Thanks to the many who then tested these recipes, and celebrated them in potlucks.

A host of friends and strangers shared ideas and questions and encouragement, especially vendors at the Regina Farmers' Market. The folks at St. James United Church have given unfailing patience and encouragement and practical help, keeping this journey on the road. The community board of the Every Bite Project has advised and acted when needed. Deana Driver pointed us to the book's title – "that's it!" Computer wizard Dan Pearson saved the dream through various crises (along with grandsons Marshall and Piper).

Thanks to those who read parts or all of the emerging text, who applied their various skills and expertise and struggled with improvements. The list includes Louise Burns-Murray, Ruth Card, Catherine Folnovic, Beryl Forgay, Evelyn Gay, Laureen Graham, Ruth Hollis,

Bev Lundahl, Colleen Mahoney, Maureen McKenzie, Virginia McKenzie, Charlotte Miller, Verda Petry, Catherine Robertson, Florence Stratton, Ann Verrall and Elizabeth Verrall, as well as professionals who answered questions. Storytellers Laura Sundberg, Kristine Beer, Jordan Fieseler, Sr. Elaine Weisgerber, Eleanor Brass, Naomi Hunter and Trevor Herriot enrich us. Young Regina artist Erika Folnovic charms with her perceptive illustrations. Thank you, each one. Special gratitude goes to Maureen Huot. From the beginning, her passion and insight bolstered mine; her creativity enlivened our ideas. Special gratitude goes also to Pauline Ferland – for reading each successive version over the two years, adding the metric measurements, and most important, for lending a listening ear.

This has been a gleaning adventure – gleaning ideas and help from an innumerable host of people, young, old and in-between; from writers and film-makers, from the internet and our faithful CBC. All helped create the vision which impelled the author, and the Book forward. The wondrous power in the universe has been surrounding and challenging and upholding us all – and the Book. We give thanks.

The Every Bite Project gratefully acknowledges the financial support of Individuals, and of the following organizations:

Healthy Horizons

Saskatchewan Council for International Cooperation (SCIC) www.earthbeat.sk.ca

Kairos Regina

St. James United Church, Regina www.stjamesunitedregina.com

Regina Public Interest Research Group (RPIRG) www.rpirg.org

The Every Bite Project

This book is part of a larger project to inform and transform lives. Sales of the book will generate seed money for the on-going journey of the Every Bite Project: community gardening; cooking classes based on the ideas and recipes in this book; and outreach workshops.

The theme *"Every Bite Affects the World"* is a reminder that our choices have consequences. In the same way, many positive actions can create a garden of opportunities to bring health and well-being to others. The gardening project is in partnership with other Regina groups that are committed to life-giving purposes. The garden and the cooking classes will bring together partners from the nutrition, self-help, ecological, anti-poverty and church sectors along with folk from the general community to make change one bite and one person at a time. We hope that this guide will enable you to be part of a world-wide movement of people dedicated to personal, communal and ecological health and well-being. Creating and re-creating potential and power is all around us. Let's tap into it and be a force for life.

Laura Sundberg for the Every Bite Project Board of Directors.

www.everybite.net